Good Housekeeping

ULTIMATE YEAR PLANNER

CONTENTS

FOREWORD

Which of the four seasons is your favourite? Spring, when nature bursts into life and anything seems possible, or those heady days of a golden summer, full of sunshine and holidays by the sea? Perhaps you long for the cosiness that winter brings, or maybe you're happiest kicking through autumn leaves and carving pumpkins for Halloween?

Here at *Good Housekeeping*, we like to say that spring stirs, summer sings, autumn whispers and in winter everything stands still - although as Christmas is one of our busiest times in the office, that's not exactly true! What our experts do know is how to get the best out of each season, whether that means planning, planting or pruning your garden; the Tried, Tested, Trusted recipes to cook; what to wear; how to care for your health; the crafts to make; and the household jobs to do, from decluttering to decorating. So, we hope that this, our first-ever year planner, will help you to get organised - and we've kept the diary pages free from days of the week so that you can start using them whenever you like. Because everything is housekeeping, and housekeeping is everything!

THE *GOOD HOUSEKEEPING* TEAM

SPRING

With the first rays of sunshine, nature bursts
into life, birds sing, flowers bloom and we
turn our thoughts to the year ahead…

Bring on spring with its brighter days, bluebells and blossom. Or, as poet Christina Rossetti described it: 'When life's alive in everything.' Finally, nature shakes off shivery winter and gives us the green light to feel more cheerful. If there's one word synonymous with the season, it's renewal. And if there's one overriding emotion, it's optimism.

We've hunkered down during winter, much like the hibernating hedgehogs and dormice. It's time to come out of our cocoons, nudge the clocks forward and see the world with fresh eyes. To spring-clean the cupboards. To decorate our homes with bright yellow daffodils and a lick of paint. To weed the garden, walk in the countryside and watch lambs playing in the fields.

Spring is the perfect time to let go of what you no longer need, by releasing old habits and emotions that no longer serve you. ⤶

March, April, May. The spring months are filled with celebrations, such as Shrove Tuesday, Mothering Sunday and Passover. May also sees two bank holidays. The first – the Early May Bank Holiday – is associated with May Day, a traditional folk festival marked by Morris and maypole dancing.

With so much to celebrate, it's time to get together with our family and friends. Handtied bouquets are gifted, glasses are raised and special meals are prepared to be shared (hello, asparagus – we've missed you). This is the season that's all about healthy eating and heartfelt entertaining. Enjoy fresh flavours and try new recipes. Sprinkle mint over peas just popped from their pods, slather Jersey Royals with salted butter and bake zesty lemon drizzle cakes.

Easter is one of the UK's most important religious festivals, with Good Friday commemorating the crucifixion of Jesus Christ, and Easter Sunday the Resurrection. The long weekend encourages fun with family and friends. Hide eggs in the garden for an Easter egg hunt. Make a pretty wreath for your front door. And embrace the excuse to enjoy plenty of chocolate!

While the dates for the two Eid festivals change

> '**WITH SO MUCH TO CELEBRATE, IT'S TIME FOR US TO GET TOGETHER WITH OUR FAMILY AND FRIENDS**'

each year, most recently the celebrations have occurred in spring. Baklava is a fitting gift, representing sweetness and abundance.

Warmer weather means putting woollies and heavy coats into storage (hooray!), or at least in the back of the wardrobe. And beauty-wise, it's time to polish up your act, exfoliating skin that's been under wraps all winter and prepping feet for sandals.

The garden beckons, too. Let's clear the decks – prune shrubs and hedges, hoe the soil and sow seeds for summer. If it's inspiration you're after, you'll get plenty from the RHS Chelsea Flower Show, the haute couture of the gardening world.

Festival season starts now, too. Check out The Hay Festival, held annually in the 'book town' of Hay-on-Wye, Wales, with its focus on literature and the arts. It's your chance to engage with some of the world's greatest writers, poets, philosophers, comedians and musicians.

Spring is the perfect time to start letting go of what you no longer need, maybe by treating your home to a determined declutter. Turn the page. Be open to new experiences. Enjoy a fresh sense of liberation. ∎

PLANNER

Dates to remember

Make a note of any birthdays, holidays, celebrations or appointments you have in the months of March, April and May

Spring goals

1
2
3
4
5

Notes

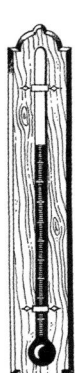

Did you know?

The seasons start at different times, depending on how they're marked. Meteorological seasons are based on annual temperature cycles within the Gregorian calendar, so March, April and May are always considered spring. Astronomical seasons are based on the Earth's position in relation to the sun, which means the dates of the two solstices (winter and summer) and two equinoxes (spring and autumn) change slightly every year. There are also 10 phenological seasons defined by the life cycle events of specific plants, animals and birds – so 'early spring', for example, starts with the emergence of snowdrops and ends when the willow tree flowers.

SPRING IN NUMBERS

626

The number of sunshine hours during the UK's sunniest spring in 2020.

9

The number of days earlier spring starts now compared with 25 years ago.

8°C

How much warmer it is inside a daffodil trumpet compared with the outside – no wonder bees love to buzz around inside them!

6,000

Pieces of moss, lichen and cobwebs expertly woven into a long-tailed tits nest.

2 mph

The speed at which scientists calculate spring travels from the southwest to the northeast of the UK – the equivalent of a leisurely stroll!

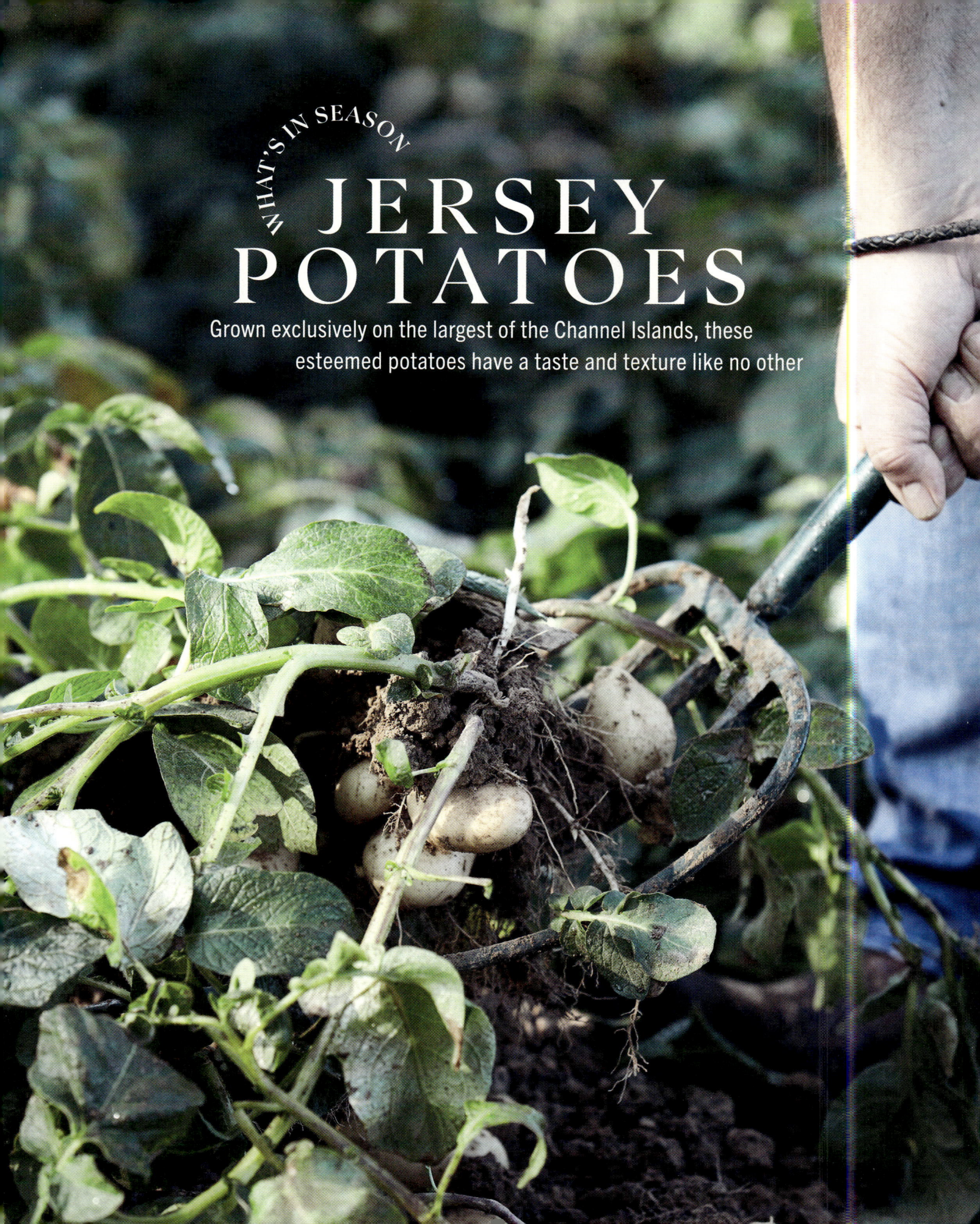

JERSEY POTATOES

Grown exclusively on the largest of the Channel Islands, these esteemed potatoes have a taste and texture like no other

SPUDS YOU LIKE

Parma ham, Champagne... and potatoes?
An unlikely addition to a list of fine foods,
but like the cured meat from Italy and
fizz from France, Jersey Royals have a
protected designation of origin status
(PDO), which means that their Channel
Islands authenticity is guaranteed. These
kidney-shaped, waxy spuds are around
from April to June, and their creamy
texture and nutty flavour is due to the
rich soil, temperate sea air and Jersey
seaweed that's used as a natural fertiliser.
Their papery skin is chock-full of flavour
and high in vitamin C, so there's no need
to peel before cooking – just give them a
good scrub. Jersey Royals are arguably at
their very best simply boiled and drenched
in herby butter, but roasting also works well.
Try parboiling until just soft, lightly crushing
with the back of a spoon, then roasting,
drizzled with plenty of olive oil. Their waxy
texture also makes them the perfect
potato for a salad. ❧

GH TIP

Check your fish is sustainably caught by looking for the Marine Stewardship Council logo.

CRUSHED JERSEY ROYAL, ROASTED RADISH AND COD TRAYBAKE

Let the oven do the work with this fresh and seasonal traybake. To speed up the recipe, you could cook your potatoes in a pan of salted boiling water until just tender, before roasting.

Hands-on time: 20min.
Cooking time:
about 55min.
Serves 4

Ingredients
750g Jersey Royals
2½tbsp olive oil
150g radishes, trimmed and halved
250g asparagus, ends trimmed and roughly chopped
1 lemon, sliced into wedges
2tbsp capers, drained
100g fresh or frozen peas
4 chunky cod fillets, roughly 125g each
75g tartar sauce

1. Preheat oven to 200°C (180°C fan) mark 6. In a large roasting tin, toss the potatoes, 2tbsp oil and seasoning. Cook for 30min, or until beginning to crisp up.

2. Remove from the oven and lightly crush using a potato masher or fork. Add the radishes, asparagus and lemon wedges, and mix through. Return to the oven for 10min.

3. Remove from the oven again, sprinkle over the capers and peas and lay over the cod fillets. Brush the cod with the remaining ½tbsp oil and season well. Cook for 15min, or until the fish is just cooked and the potatoes are golden. Dollop on or serve with the tartar sauce.

PER SERVING *400cals, 29g protein, 13g fat (2g saturates), 37g carbs (8g total sugars), 7g fibre*

14

FOODWISE

The onset of spring is always a relief in the kitchen. After the seeming endlessness of comfort-food cooking through winter, things suddenly start to feel a lot lighter and less time consuming. Whether you're buying bundles of fresh asparagus or harvesting your first crop of broad beans, it's hard not to get excited about experimenting with all that lovely seasonal produce. And with the prospect of eating outside just around the corner, what's not to love about springing into action and trying a few new recipes?

IN SEASON

PURPLE SPROUTING BROCCOLI
One of the first of the spring crops, this pretty vegetable is in peak season between February and April. Look out for firm stems, dark green leaves and deep purple florets.

BROAD BEANS
The first beans, harvested in May, tend to be smaller and sweeter and you can usually get away without double-podding them. The season runs throughout the summer, though, and beans harvested later definitely benefit from being popped out of their papery skins after blanching.

ASPARAGUS
The true A-lister of spring, British asparagus has a very short season that runs from the end of April through to Midsummer's Day in June. Look for firm stems and prolong their life by standing them in water in the fridge, or wrapping stems in damp paper.

WATERCRESS
May is the official start of watercress season, which runs all the way through to October. High temperatures can make watercress bitter, so spring really is the best time to enjoy these vibrant, peppery leaves.

RADISHES
Their season typically runs from May through to early autumn, but radishes are at their peak in May and June. Part of the mustard family, they're famed for their crisp texture and distinctive peppery taste. Keep the tops — they're great in salads or sautéed.

DID YOU KNOW?

ASPARAGUS IS KNOWN AS THE 'USAIN BOLT OF THE VEGETABLE WORLD' AS IT CAN GROW UP TO 10CM IN A SINGLE DAY.

DO A...
Kitchen clearout

Over the winter months, storecupboards and freezers can become overrun as we make up for a dearth of seasonal fruit and vegetables (if you're still hoarding a load of stuff you overbought during the festive season, you're probably not alone!). Spring is the perfect time of year to have a proper sort-out of storecupboards, the freezer — and that top shelf of the fridge where random jars of who-knows-what go to die. Here are our top decluttering tips:
✦ Check expiry dates and get rid of anything well past its best before or use-by label.
✦ Consider donating unwanted — but in-date — food to a food bank.
✦ Group similar items so it's easier to see what you have, and invest in baskets or containers to store them together.
✦ Think about having a labelled drawer in your fridge and freezer for items near their expiry date so that you can see at a glance what you should use up first.

3 WAYS TO SERVE SPRING ON A PLATE

Quick and easy ideas to make the most of seasonal produce

A typically French way to enjoy radishes; just wash, top and tail and present on a board with some softened butter and sea salt. Swipe the radish through the butter, then sprinkle with salt before eating.

For a speedy side to accompany spring lamb, sauté finely chopped anchovies in butter for a couple of minutes with lots of cracked black pepper, then stir through blanched purple sprouting broccoli and toss to coat.

Whizz ricotta with Greek yoghurt and lemon zest and spoon on to a serving plate. Top with blanched asparagus and finish with lemon juice, extra virgin oil and toasted hazelnuts. Serve this great sharing dish with crusty bread.

A DELICIOUS EASTER

Gather friends and family around the table to celebrate with a spring feast, full of delicious seasonal flavours

GH TIP

Swap the parsley and pine nuts for any other herbs or nuts you prefer; mint and pistachio would be a particularly tasty alternative.

MENU

FOR 8

*Pea and Courgette Soup
with Feta and Dill Scones*

*Artichoke Stuffed
Leg of Lamb with
Red Wine Gravy*

*Dressed Baby Carrots
with Crispy Shallots*

*Jersey Royal
and Fennel Salad*

*Beans, Greens and
Roasted Cherry Tomatoes*

*Leek and Asparagus
Galette (Vegetarian)*

*Rhubarb
Frangipane Tart*

ARTICHOKE STUFFED LEG OF LAMB WITH RED WINE GRAVY

Ask your butcher to bone and butterfly the lamb for you to make easy work of this decadent rolled leg, generously stuffed with artichoke hearts, pine nuts, lemon zest and garlic, served with a simple roasting tin gravy.

Hands-on time: 35min, plus resting. Cooking time: about 1hr 15min. Serves 8

FOR THE LAMB
2 onions, roughly chopped
2 celery sticks, roughly chopped
2 carrots, trimmed and roughly chopped
2 bay leaves
2kg boned and rolled leg of lamb (ask the butcher to save the bones)
75g fresh breadcrumbs
125g marinated artichoke hearts (drained weight), roughly chopped
50g pine nuts, toasted
Small bunch parsley, leaves picked and finely chopped
4 garlic cloves
Finely grated zest and juice 1 lemon, keep separate
1 large egg, beaten
1tbsp olive oil
FOR THE GRAVY
2tbsp plain flour
150ml red wine
500ml hot chicken or vegetable stock
2tbsp redcurrant jelly
YOU WILL ALSO NEED
Kitchen string

1. Preheat oven to 220°C (200°C fan) mark 7. For the lamb, in a large, sturdy roasting tin mix the onions, celery, carrots, bay leaves and lamb bones (if using). Weigh the lamb and calculate cooking time, allowing 15min per 450g for pink meat, or longer if you prefer your lamb more well done.
2. For the stuffing, in a medium bowl mix the breadcrumbs, artichokes, pine nuts, parsley, 2 crushed garlic cloves, the lemon zest, egg and plenty of seasoning.
3. Arrange the lamb on a board, skin-side down. Gently cut into the leg at the thickest part and open out like a book, without cutting through the meat to the board. Cover with baking parchment or clingfilm and bash a little with a rolling pin to flatten evenly.
4. Spread stuffing on top, leaving a slight border around the edges. Fold the shortest edge over to cover some of the stuffing, then roll up the meat from the folded edge and secure with kitchen string at 3cm intervals.
5. Finely slice the remaining 2 garlic cloves. Make a few slits in the meat with the tip of a sharp knife and push in the garlic slices. Sit lamb in the roasting tin on top of the vegetables. In a small bowl mix the oil and lemon juice. Brush over the lamb and season.
6. Cook for calculated time, reducing the oven to 200°C (180°C fan) mark 6 after 20min.
7. Remove lamb to a board, cover with a double layer of foil and leave to rest in a warm place for at least 20min (up to 40min).
8. Meanwhile, make the gravy. Carefully remove and discard bones (if using). Put tin over medium hob heat and spoon off excess fat. Stir in the flour, mashing the vegetables as you go. Cook, stirring, for 1min. Gradually stir in the wine (scraping up all the sticky bits from the base of the tin) and bubble for a few min. Stir in the stock and simmer until thickened, then stir in the redcurrant jelly.
9. Add any resting juices from the lamb to gravy tin and check seasoning. Strain into a warmed jug. Serve with the lamb.
PER SERVING *574cals, 56g protein, 29g fat (10g saturates), 17g carbs (7g total sugars), 3g fibre* ➻

GET AHEAD

Prepare lamb to end of step 5 up to a day ahead, cover and chill. To serve, uncover and allow lamb to come up to room temperature for 30min before completing recipe.

PEA AND COURGETTE SOUP WITH FETA AND DILL SCONES

A deliciously comforting bowl of vibrant spring soup, served with warm scones for dipping. This would also make a lovely light lunch on its own.

Hands-on time: 30min. Cooking time: about 50min. Serves 8

FOR THE SOUP
2tbsp extra virgin olive oil, plus extra to drizzle
1 bunch spring onions, trimmed and chopped
2 garlic cloves, sliced
2 courgettes, trimmed and roughly chopped
300g floury potatoes, peeled and roughly chopped
1 litre vegetable stock
400g frozen peas
Large handful dill, roughly chopped, plus extra to garnish
FOR THE SCONES
450g self-raising flour, plus extra to dust
1tsp baking powder
100g unsalted butter, chilled and cubed
10g dill, finely chopped
150g feta, crumbled, plus extra to garnish
1 large egg
200ml whole milk

1. For the soup, heat the oil in a large pan over medium heat and cook the spring onions and garlic for 5min, until lightly golden. Add the courgettes and cook for 5min, until just starting to colour. Stir in the potatoes, stock and some seasoning. Bring to the boil, then reduce heat and simmer for 15min, or until the potatoes are just tender.

GET AHEAD

Make soup to end of step 2 up to 2 days ahead. Cool, cover and chill. Make scones up to 3hr ahead. To serve, complete recipe, reheating scones in oven preheated to 160°C (140°C fan) mark 3 for 5min.

Add the peas and simmer for 5min. Remove from heat.
2. Stir in the dill, then carefully blend (in batches, if needed) until smooth. Return to the empty pan and check seasoning. Set aside.
3. For the scones, preheat oven to 200°C (180°C fan) mark 6 and put in a large baking sheet to heat up. In a large bowl, whisk the flour, baking powder and 1tsp fine salt until combined. Add the butter and rub in using your fingertips until the mixture resembles breadcrumbs. Briefly mix in the dill and 100g feta.
4. In a small jug, whisk the egg and

'IF YOU DON'T HAVE FETA, THE SCONES WOULD WORK AS WELL WITH SOME GOAT'S CHEESE OR CHEDDAR'

milk, until combined. Make a well in the centre of the dry ingredients and pour in most of the egg mixture (reserving 2tbsp). Using a cutlery knife, gently mix until the dough comes together. Knead briefly in the bowl to make a soft, but not sticky, dough.
5. Lightly flour a work surface, tip out the dough and pat out to a rough circle, about 2.5cm thick. Cut into 8 equal triangles and arrange on a sheet of baking parchment, spacing apart. Brush reserved milk mixture over the tops of the scones and sprinkle over remaining 50g feta.
6. Transfer scones (on parchment) to the preheated baking sheet and cook for 18-20min, or until risen and lightly golden.
7. To serve, reheat soup until piping hot. Divide between 8 bowls, garnish with feta, a drizzle of oil and dill. Serve with the warm scones.
PER SERVING *527cals, 17g protein, 23g fat (12g saturates), 59g carbs (6g total sugars), 7g fibre*

GET AHEAD

Prepare to end of step 2 up to a day ahead. Cool, cover and chill filling. To serve, allow pastry to soften at room temperature for 15min before completing recipe.

LEEK AND ASPARAGUS GALETTE

Sweet, tender leeks encased in crumbly hazelnut pastry make for a fabulous vegetarian main course.

Hands-on time: 30min, plus chilling and cooling. Cooking time: about 45min. Serves 8

FOR THE HAZELNUT PASTRY
75g blanched hazelnuts
225g plain flour, plus extra to dust
150g unsalted butter, chilled and cubed
1 large egg, beaten
FOR THE FILLING
3 medium leeks
40g unsalted butter
1 echalion shallot, finely sliced
6 thyme sprigs, leaves picked
1tsp Dijon mustard
200ml double cream
50g mature Cheddar, grated
75g vegetarian Italian-style hard cheese, finely grated
225g asparagus spears, trimmed and halved lengthways
1tbsp olive oil
1tbsp milk

1. For the pastry, in a food processor, whizz the hazelnuts until finely ground. Add the flour, butter and a pinch of salt. Pulse until it resembles breadcrumbs. Add the egg and pulse until the pastry comes together. Tip on to a work surface, shape into a disc, wrap and chill for 30min.
2. Meanwhile, make the filling. Trim, halve lengthways and finely slice 2 of the leeks. Melt the butter in a large frying pan over low-medium heat and cook the leeks, shallot, thyme and a pinch of salt for 8-10min, or until softened. Remove from heat and stir in the mustard, cream, Cheddar, 60g hard cheese and some seasoning. Leave to cool completely.
3. Meanwhile, trim and slice the remaining leek into long strips, roughly the same width and length as the asparagus. Add to a large bowl with the asparagus and oil and toss to coat.
4. Lightly flour a large sheet of baking parchment and roll out pastry to a rough 40cm circle. Slide pastry (still on parchment) on to a large baking sheet. Spread the filling over the pastry, leaving a 5cm border around the edges. Top with the asparagus and leek mixture. Fold in the pastry edges to slightly cover the filling (don't worry if it looks a little rustic). Chill for 30min.
5. Preheat oven to 200°C (180°C fan) mark 6. Brush folded pastry with milk and scatter remaining grated hard cheese over the filling. Cook for 30-35min, or until the pastry is golden and crisp at the edges. Leave to cool for a few min on the sheet, then transfer to a board or serving plate. Serve.
PER SERVING 551cals, 13g protein, 43g fat (30g saturates), 22g carbs (3g total sugars), 5g fibre ➤

GET AHEAD

For the carrots, make dressing up to
a day ahead; cover and chill. Make
shallots up to 2 days ahead; keep in
an airtight container lined with
kitchen paper at room temperature.
For the potatoes, cook and make the
salsa verde up to a day ahead. Cool,
cover and chill separately.
For the beans and tomatoes, prepare
to end of step 2 up to 3hr ahead.
Cover tomatoes and beans separately
and set aside at room temperature.

DRESSED BABY CARROTS & CRISPY SHALLOTS

You could cheat and use shop-bought crispy onions, if you prefer.

Hands-on time 15min. Cooking time about 30min. Serves 8

1kg baby carrots, scrubbed and trimmed
2tbsp extra virgin olive oil
2tsp cumin seeds
1tbsp coriander seeds, crushed
½tsp dried chilli flakes
1tbsp nigella seeds
150ml vegetable oil
1 echalion shallot, finely sliced into rings
FOR THE DRESSING
¼tsp Dijon mustard
3tbsp extra virgin olive oil
Juice 1 lemon
1tbsp finely chopped dill
1tbsp finely chopped parsley

1. Preheat oven to 200°C (180°C fan) mark 6. In a large roasting tin, mix the carrots, olive oil, spices (except the nigella seeds) and some seasoning. Arrange in a single layer and cook for 25min, or until tender and golden. Scatter over the nigella seeds and return to the oven for 5min.
2. Meanwhile, heat the vegetable oil in a medium pan over medium-high heat for 2-3min. Fry the shallot rings in batches, until golden and crispy. Remove with a slotted spoon to a plate lined with kitchen paper and sprinkle with salt.
3. For the dressing, in a small bowl whisk the mustard, oil, lemon juice and some seasoning, then whisk in the herbs.
4. Empty the carrots on to a serving plate, drizzle over the dressing and scatter over the crispy shallots. Serve.

PER SERVING 142cals, 2g protein, 11g fat (2g saturates), 7g carbs (7g total sugars), 5g fibre

JERSEY ROYAL & FENNEL SALAD

Tossing these in the salsa verde while warm helps them absorb more flavour.

Hands-on time 10min. Cooking time about 25min. Serves 8

750g Jersey Royal potatoes, halved if large
1 fennel bulb, finely sliced, fronds reserved, if present
Juice ½ lemon
FOR THE SALSA VERDE
40g parsley, finely chopped
40g mint, leaves picked and finely chopped
1 garlic clove, finely chopped
6 cornichons, finely chopped
2tsp nonpareille capers, finely chopped
4 anchovy fillets in olive oil, drained and finely chopped
1tbsp Dijon mustard
2tbsp red wine vinegar
4tbsp extra virgin olive oil

1. Bring a large pan of salted water to the boil. Add the potatoes and simmer for 20min, or until tender. Drain and leave to steam-dry for 1min.
2. Meanwhile, in a large bowl, mix all the salsa verde ingredients with some seasoning. In a separate bowl, toss the fennel, lemon juice and a pinch of salt.
3. Add potatoes to the salsa verde bowl and toss to coat. Add fennel and toss again gently. Empty into a serving dish, top with any reserved fronds. Serve.
PER SERVING 135cals, 3g protein, 6g fat (1g saturates), 16g carbs (2g total sugars), 3g fibre

BEANS, GREENS & ROASTED CHERRY TOMATOES

You could also try using cannellini or butter beans.

Hands-on time 15min. Cooking time about 50min. Serves 8

300g cherry tomatoes on the vine, snipped into smaller bunches
2tbsp extra virgin olive oil, plus extra to drizzle
2 echalion shallots, finely sliced
3 garlic cloves, finely sliced
½tsp dried chilli flakes
150ml white wine
2 x 400g tins haricot beans
250g spring greens, finely shredded
Juice 1 lemon

1. Preheat oven to 200°C (180°C fan) mark 6. Put tomatoes in a small roasting tin and drizzle over 1tbsp oil. Season and cook in oven for 10-15min, or until starting to split and soften.
2. Meanwhile, heat remaining 1tbsp oil in a large, deep frying pan (that has a lid) over medium heat. Cook the shallots for 8min, until softened. Stir in the garlic and chilli flakes and cook for 2min. Pour in the wine and bubble for 6-7min, until reduced. Empty in the beans and their juices and season. Bring to a simmer, then reduce heat and cook for 20min, stirring occasionally, until thickened and 'creamy'.
3. Stir in the spring greens and a splash of water, cover with the lid and cook for 7-8min, or until tender. Remove from the heat, stir in the lemon juice and check seasoning. Empty into a serving bowl and top with the roasted tomatoes and a drizzle of oil. Serve.
PER SERVING 129cals, 6g protein, 4g fat (1g saturates), 12g carbs (3g total sugars), 7g fibre ➥

RHUBARB FRANGIPANE TART

Dainty pink stems of rhubarb nestled in sweet frangipane – the prettiest dessert to end any celebration meal.

Hands-on time: 45min, plus chilling and cooling. Cooking time: about 1hr 55min. Serves 8

FOR THE PASTRY
300g plain flour, plus extra to dust
50g icing sugar
175g unsalted butter, chilled and cubed
Finely grated zest 1 orange
1 large egg yolk
FOR THE FRANGIPANE
225g unsalted butter, softened
225g caster sugar, plus 1tbsp extra to sprinkle
3 large eggs
150g ground almonds
50g plain flour
250g rhubarb, trimmed

1. For the pastry, in a food processor, pulse the flour, icing sugar and a pinch of fine salt until combined. Add the butter and orange zest, and pulse until the mixture resembles fine breadcrumbs. Alternatively, rub the butter into the flour mixture using your fingers.
2. Add the egg yolk and 1-2tbsp ice-cold water and pulse/mix until pastry begins to clump together. Tip on to a work surface, shape into a disc, wrap and chill for 30min.
3. Lightly dust pastry with flour and roll out between 2 sheets of baking parchment to a rough 35cm circle. Carefully peel off top parchment and invert into a rough 24cm round, loose-bottomed fluted tart tin. Remove parchment and gently ease pastry into place to line tin neatly. Trim edges to neaten and prick base all over with a fork. Chill for 10min.
4. Preheat oven to 180°C (160°C fan) mark 4. Line pastry case with 1 of the baking parchment sheets and fill with baking beans. Bake for 18min, or until the pastry sides are set. Carefully lift out parchment and beans and return tin to the oven for 5min, or until the base feels sandy to the touch and is lightly golden. Set aside.
5. For the frangipane, in a food processor, whizz the butter and sugar until light and creamy. Add the eggs and whizz again until combined. Add the ground almonds and flour; pulse until just combined. Alternatively, beat the butter and sugar using a handheld electric whisk, then beat in the eggs and fold in the ground almonds and flour using a metal spoon.
6. Scrape frangipane into the pastry case (still in tin) and gently spread to level. Halve the rhubarb lengthways and cut on the diagonal into 2-3cm pieces. Arrange on top of the frangipane, packing it in tightly as the rhubarb will shrink on baking. Sprinkle over the 1tbsp sugar and bake for 1hr 15min-1hr 30min (covering with foil if catching) or until frangipane is set.
7. Leave to cool in the tin for 10min, then transfer to a serving plate, or wire rack (if not serving immediately). Serve warm or at room temperature with crème fraîche, if you like.
PER SERVING (without crème fraîche) 776cals, 13g protein, 51g fat (26g saturates), 65g carbs (36g total sugars), 2g fibre ■

'RHUBARB PAIRS WELL WITH PISTACHIO, SO TRY GROUND PISTACHIOS INSTEAD OF GROUND ALMONDS IN THE FRANGIPANE'

GET AHEAD

Bake pastry case up to a day ahead. Cool completely then store (still in tin) in an airtight container at room temperature. Complete recipe to serve. Alternatively, make up to 6hr ahead and serve at room temperature or reheat in an oven preheated to 160°C (140°C fan) mark 3 for 10min.

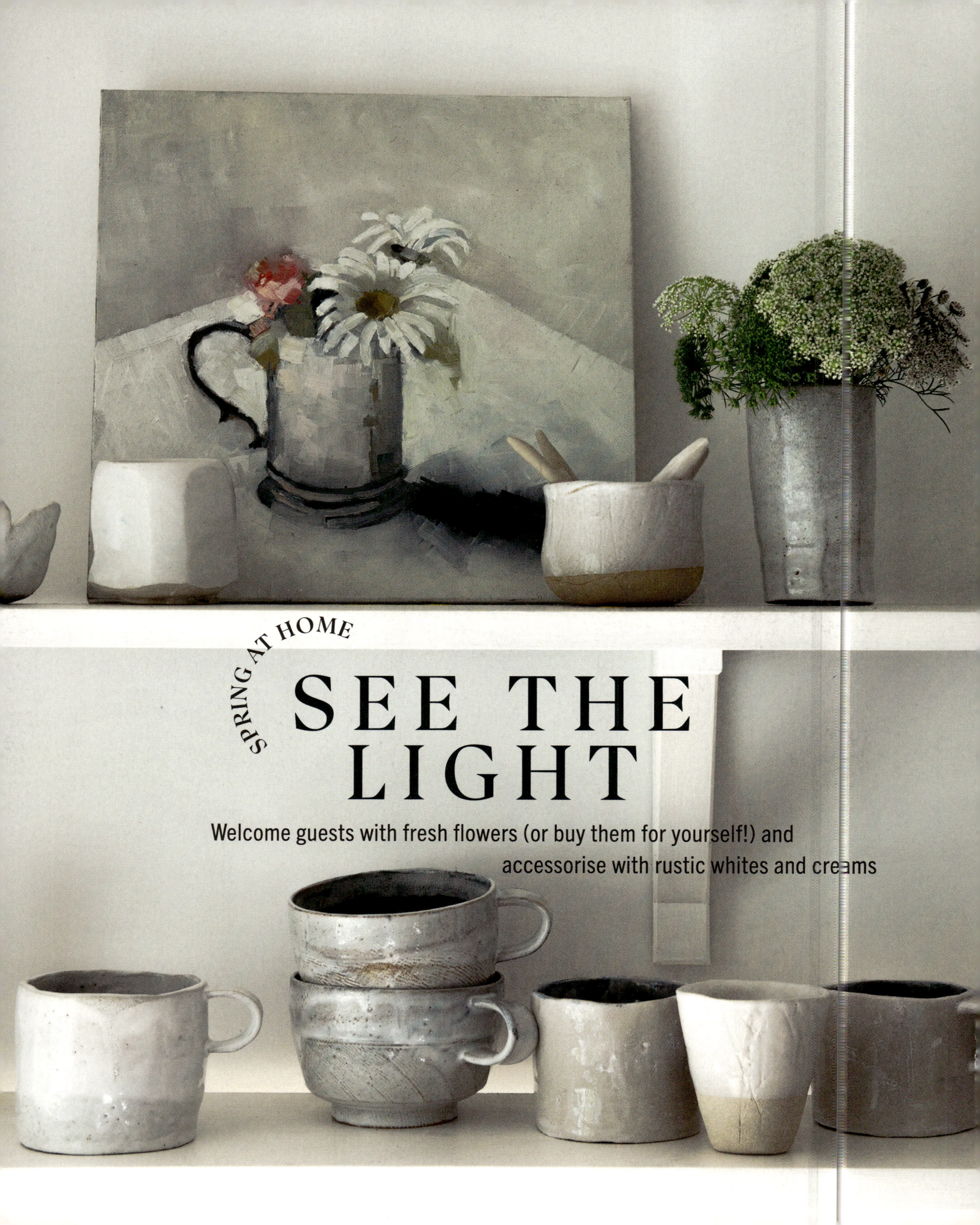

SPRING AT HOME

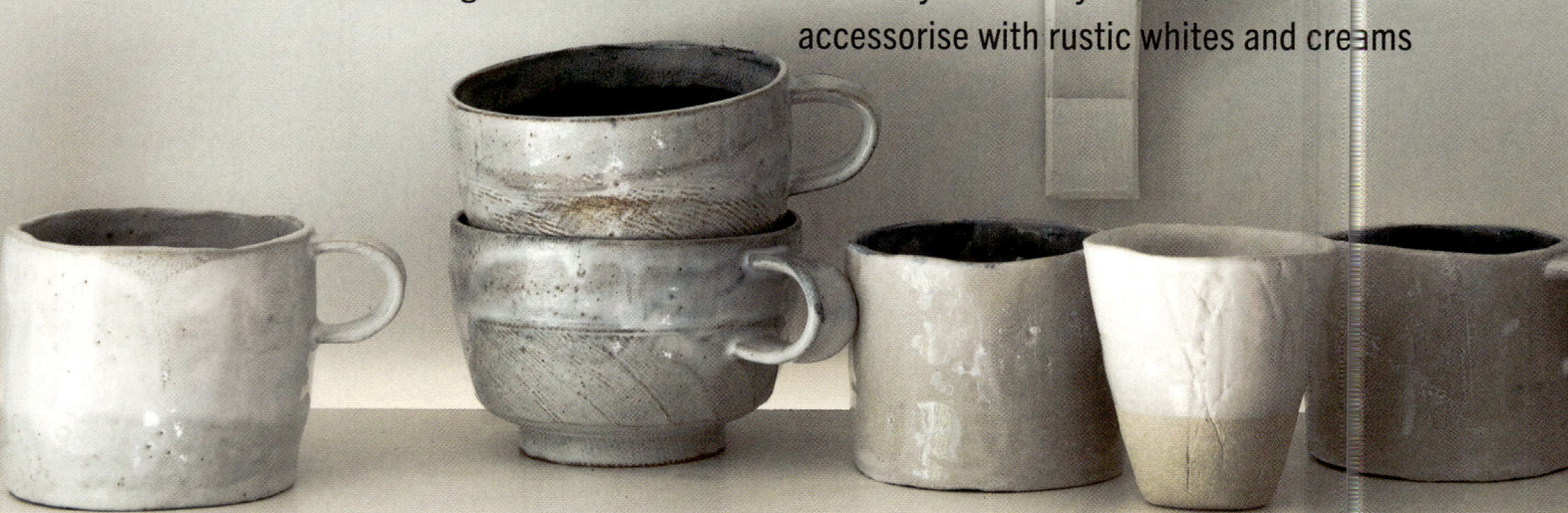

SEE THE LIGHT

Welcome guests with fresh flowers (or buy them for yourself!) and accessorise with rustic whites and creams

GH TIP

Vintage furniture creates a shabby chic look, which works well with a light spring palette. Look for pieces that are good quality but still full of character and charm. ❧

PRETTY LITTLE THINGS

Small collections of items, or vignettes, placed carefully throughout your home will add a finishing touch that can be changed to match the season.

On a mantelpiece, add decorative mirrors to reflect light around the room and fill vases with spring blooms. But why stop at one? Experiment with different containers, mixing and matching sizes and materials to create a triptych. One could have a single shade of flower and another, a sprig or two of green leaves. On coffee tables, create a statement with centrepieces – try bowls filled with large flowerheads such as hydrangeas or peonies.

Open shelving or flat surfaces are the perfect place for displaying tactile objects – try ceramics stacked at different heights. And don't think you have to frame and hang every piece of art – try propping pictures against walls for a more relaxed vibe. Instead of stashing away pretty accessories, such as straw hats or jewellery, use them to decorate forgotten corners of your home. ❧

GH TIP

You don't have to spend a
fortune on flowers to achieve
a stylish display — grow
cottage garden favourites,
such as feverfew and Queen
Anne's lace, so you can cut
your own flowers.

COLOUR CODE

Soft, off-white shades accentuate light — and are the perfect way to refresh your walls after the darkness of winter.

FALLING FOR FABRIC

Draping material over chairs, adding soft throws or investing in easy to change slip covers will immediately add a more relaxed vibe — switch up darker shades for paler fabrics in spring. Adding new shades or patterns with textiles is the easiest and quickest way to bring life to worn-out pieces of furniture and change the look and feel of your space. Covers or sheets made from synthetic fabrics are tighter-fitting (and harder-wearing) but natural fabrics, such as cotton and linen, are looser so will give a more laid-back and romantic feel — especially in bedrooms.

Add an extra layer of softness with flounced or pleated accessories. Go large with a pendant lampshade to create a boho look, but choose a lightweight textile so the shade doesn't overwhelm the room. An added bonus is that a lighter fabric will gently diffuse light, further accentuating a laid-back vibe.

If you love plain bedlinen, add a gentle focal point with a few oversized cushions edged with frills, or in a pretty pattern, such as broderie anglaise, to keep the romance alive. ■

HOMEWISE

Who can resist bringing a touch of spring inside in the shape of fresh flowers? As the sunshine starts to illuminate our homes, don't be afraid to give walls or furniture a fresh lick of paint and swap out dark cushions and throws for lighter shades. There's no need to do a full spring reset, though. Go from room to room, swapping out one key piece to make a visual difference – a new lampshade, piece of art or rug. No need to buy new, either – swapping pieces from one room to another will give you a similar impact.

HANG A WREATH

A spring wreath hung on your front door is a lovely way to bid farewell to winter. If you opt for real flowers and greenery, spray your wreath regularly to keep it fresh. For a low-maintenance option, use good-quality silk blooms and foliage.

COFFEE-TABLE CHIC

Assemble a pretty display for a coffee table or sideboard. First, decide on your colour Palette, then select a tray in a size that fits one third of the space. Place a pot of forced flowers such as hyacinths or narcissus, or a vase of flowers, in one corner and add a couple of small books (extra points if they have a floral or spring theme!) beside it to add height then place a small, scented candle on top. If you have a bigger, multi-wick candle, place it next to the books and pop an ornament on top of those instead.

Spring buy

A new vase. A jug is your least formal option and perfect for wild flowers. A bud vase is for a few short sprigs, such as sweetpeas. With boat-shaped vases, you can play with height and scale (use a flower frog to keep blooms in place). A tulipiere has multiple spouts. Made for tulips, it looks just as lovely with other flowers, too.

Home scents

Look for honeysuckle (a sweet fragrance with hints of honey), the earthy green tones of gardenia and the muskier notes of jasmine.

Easter decor

Painted eggs look pretty hung from a 'tree' in the middle of your table. Create one using branches of pussy willow, and attach your eggs using pastel-coloured ribbons.

Good Housekeeping Institute
TRIED ★ TESTED ★ TRUSTED

TO-DO LIST

Every year, the GHI keeps millions of people safe from the crushing disappointment of a bad purchase, whether they're deliberating over their next air fryer for easy family dinners or hunting down a delicious, full-bodied red wine for their next dinner party.

At our testing facility, everything from hot sauce to slow cookers and sports bras is poked, prodded and put through its paces by experts. What Q's lab is to James Bond, the GHI is to *Good Housekeeping*!

Our team of engineers, cosmetic scientists, food developers, chemists and editors reviews thousands of products each year to bring you the very best – that's a lot of vacuuming, wiping, washing, cooking and soaking. Together, there's nothing they don't know about making a home (and your life) run smoothly. So, who better to help you put together the ultimate seasonal to-do list?

Spring at the GHI sees us finishing off our Easter taste tests and getting ready for summer. In our homes, it's a time to freshen up spaces, get ahead with the inevitable life admin, put winter clothes away and start decluttering our wardrobes.

Declutter with
THE REVERSE
HANGER TECHNIQUE

The premise of this method is simple: you reverse all the hangers on your clothes rail so they're facing the wrong way. Then, once you've worn an item, you put it back on the hanger and turn it to face the right way again. Do this for three months and by the end of spring you'll (hopefully!) see more hangers that are facing the right way than not. These are the clothes worth keeping, since they've been worn the most often.

Any clothes that are still on 'reversed' hangers should be laid out so you can look at them and ask yourself: 'If I haven't worn this for the past three months, do I really need it?'

If you still like the item (and, most importantly, it fits you), think about what you could wear it with before you put it back. If you decide to get rid of it, there are a few options to consider. You can donate pieces to local charity shops and clothes banks once cleaned. Alternatively, try selling them on sites such as Vinted or eBay. If they're damaged and beyond repair, take them to recycling centres (check with your local council to confirm locations).

It's worth applying the reverse hanger technique twice a year when you swap over your spring/summer and autumn/winter clothes to help you decluttter the full extent of your wardrobe.

Time to tidy SHOES

Start by sorting through any shoes that are stacked near the front door. Remove any that aren't worn regularly for long-term storage in your wardrobe. If any of them hurt when you wear them, get rid — it's not worth the pain! The rest can be paired up and organised with a shoe rack, or a bench with dedicated compartments. This area should be reserved for pairs that are worn daily. Try not to stack shoes directly on top of one another; the dirt from soles will rub on to the uppers. In your wardrobe, you can use single-pair shoe organisers to double the available space, and door racks if you're lacking floor space. If you're looking to buy a shoe organiser for multiple pairs, make sure you measure the space first and take into account that these often can't accommodate boots or heels. ➛

UPGRADE YOUR HANGERS

Never use wire or plastic hangers – they can distort clothes and are liable to break. Instead, invest in velvet-feel ones that take up less space, look more attractive and, most importantly, have a non-slip surface that helps to keep garments in place. Use chunkier wooden hangers for heavier garments such as coats and suits. Look for designs that have wider, rounded shoulders to better distribute the weight and keep the shape. You can also buy hangers designed for scarves and bags.

Paint fences

Paint and repair your garden fences if they're looking a little weather-worn after winter. Typically, fences need repainting every two to three years to stay in top condition. The same goes for sheds, trellises and other exposed surfaces. For the best water resistance, choose a wax-enriched formula, plan for two coats and work in smaller sections so you can recoat on the same day.

Spring-clean your inbox

Sort your emails from oldest to newest, delete what you don't need and archive anything important. Unsubscribe from newsletters and emails from brands. If you use the iOS Mail app, look for a banner at the top of emails that says 'This message is from a mailing list. Unsubscribe'. Tap that and the sender will get your 'unsubscribe' request.

Update your CV

Even if you're not actively looking for a new job, it's good practice to do this every six months, recording any new achievements. March to May tends to be a good period to seek new opportunities, as it's when many companies start their new fiscal year and begin to recruit.

Life admin

Book your key check-ups for the year in early spring so they're in the diary and won't hang around on your to-do list. These include dental check-ups, your eye test (you should get your eyes checked every two years or as often as your optician recommends) and your car service and MOT — you can sign up for text or email MOT reminders at gov.uk/mot-reminder. ■

GET AHEAD OF HAYFEVER

If you suffer with hayfever, now's the time to start thinking about prevention, as grass pollens are prevalent in April and May. Take steps to reduce the amount of pollen in your home. Leave your shoes at the door, shower when you come in and change into fresh clothes, popping your worn garments in the wash. Pollen settles on your hair and skin, so wash your bedding more regularly. An air purifier will also help to detect and trap pollen. If you're in the market for a new vacuum, look for one with a high-efficiency particulate air (HEPA) filter that traps allergens.

SPRING IN THE GARDEN

TULIP FEVER

Bulbs bloom and bring a riot of colour
to the garden as nature finally wakes up

The sight of tulips pushing their goblet-shaped heads out of the earth is a surefire sign that spring has arrived. But why settle for regulation scarlet tulips when you can have exuberant orange 'Ballerina', flame-streaked 'Prinses Irene' and dramatic 'Black Hero'? The choices – and there are so many! – are yours, but be sure to back them up with froths of acid-green euphorbias or textural bronze grasses to display them to the max.

This is also the time of year when woodland plants come out to play. Daffodils lead the way, of course, but forget-me-nots, violas, pulmonaria and primroses also make familiar mats of colour. Start by providing the partly shaded, cool conditions they favour, beneath deciduous shrubs and trees. Then, for authenticity, settle them in with a woodland-style coverlet of bark chippings. What better way to welcome spring than with a carpet of flowers? ❧

'THE LOCKET-LIKE FLOWERS OF A BLEEDING HEART
ARE SPRING SHOWSTOPPERS'

FLOWER POWER

Must-have standouts include the hellebore (right), one of the first flowers to bloom in early spring, making it a precious nectar stop for early pollinators. The deep plum of 'Blue Metallic Lady' is positively sumptuous. Plant one or two in partial shade and, in time, they'll multiply. Bleeding heart, with locket-like flowers strung across its arching stems, is another spring showstopper. It's most usually sugar pink (left), but snow-white *Lamprocapnos spectabilis* 'Alba' is preferred by purists. You'll lose it in summer but, as a reliable perennial, it will pop up next spring above ferny foliage.

Shuttlecock ferns, *Matteuccia struthiopteris*, are a great addition to the spring garden and need little attention provided they are planted in moist, dappled shade where light can filter through the lacy fronds. One plant that thrives all year round, however, is the hardy and succulent houseleek. Shown below in oversized stone bowls, they show that even the humblest of plants can look sensational when used en masse. ❧

BURIED TREASURES

Bulbs are an easy and inexpensive way to bring your garden to life in spring. If you missed out on planting last autumn, make this the time you visit gardens, and check out specialists online to note what to order for a fabulous display next year. You can also buy flowering bulbs in pots from garden centres for instant results, then drop them into borders or terracotta pots to admire on the patio. Our suggestion for fuss-free – and some of the prettiest – narcissi is to choose dwarf daffs (right) that don't flop over in spring gales, and are perfect for pots and planting beneath shrubs and trees, such as 'Hawera' and snow-white 'Thalia'.

Grape hyacinth (above left), along with forget-me-nots, make welcome ribbons of blue through the border. Choose a garden-worthy version such as Muscari 'Blue Magic'. For big, bold displays in borders and pots from mid spring onwards, nothing beats the glamour of a tulip. The hardest part of growing them? Choosing which to grow. Parrot tulip 'Professor Rontgen', top right, dazzles in spring sunlight. ➥

GH TIP

The vibrant acid green of euphorbias wakes up the garden in spring and shows tulips to perfection. Here, the frothy heads of *Euphorbia robbiae* make a textural contrast to pheasant's tail grass (*Anemanthele lessoniana*).

GH TIP

Plants that break up an expanse of paving are a great idea, especially when they include a tree. If you have space for one, copy this garden and make it an *Amelanchier*, which produces blossom in spring, black berries in summer and colourful foliage come autumn. ∎

GARDENWISE

Nature is waking up, bringing with it the delicious scent of anticipation, as leaves unfurl and blossom appears on the trees, while early-flowering clematis, camellias and magnolias mark the beginning of spring proper. It's a busy time in the garden, with the focus on preparing beds and borders, pruning summer-flowering shrubs and sowing annuals to put on a vibrant show come summer.

Early spring

Cut back deciduous grasses such as Miscanthus. For semi-evergreen grasses like ponytail (*Stipa tenuissima*), run your fingers through them to remove dead thatch. Prune buddleias back hard to about 30cm so that flowers will bloom lower down. Cut viticella clematis stems to the lowest buds, 15-30cm above soil level.

Mid-spring

Plant summer-flowering lily bulbs in deep pots, adding a handful of grit to compost to improve drainage. Try these fragrant stunners: trumpet-flowered white *Lilium regale* and speckled pink 'Stargazer'. Bury dahlia tubers in pots of moist compost, with their main stem just visible, and protect from frost. Sprinkle granular feed around the base of fruit bushes and roses.

Late spring

Pull out clumps of dead forget-me-nots, shaking them to release seed in places where you'd like them to grow. When bulbs in pots have finished flowering, plant them into the ground if you'd like them to bloom next year. Complete buying and planting trees and shrubs. Love magnolias? A great choice for a small garden or large container is the white starry-flowered *Magnolia stellata*.

Top 5: Short cuts

1. Missed out on bulb planting? Buy ready-potted bulbs in bud – crocus, hyacinth, muscari, tulips, daffodils – and either repot them or, easier still, drop them into garden pots and group them on the patio for a spring display.

2. To give yourself a money-saving head start on summer bedding, pot up 'tots' or plugs of summer bedding plants into small pots of multi-purpose compost and protect them until the danger of frost has passed.

3. Mulching borders with a 5-10cm layer of bark chippings, well-rotted manure or compost will help soil retain moisture and improve structure, benefiting plants and reducing watering later.

4. Scatter seeds of hardy annuals on to weed-free soil for a colourful summer show: pot marigolds, nigella and opium poppies are easy and speedy.

5. Push supports into soil around perennials that are inclined to flop, such as peonies, as soon as you see any signs of growth – it'll save a lot of heartache later!

GROW A HERB GARDEN

This is the best time to replenish – or start – a herb garden, in raised beds, pots or planted in the border in sunny spots. Buy small sizes because they'll grow fast and spread in a season. A good starter kit for the kitchen could feature thyme (including lemon thyme), rosemary (upright or trailing), oregano and sage. Mint grows like a weed, so keep it contained and in a shadier site.

WANT TO GIVE POTATO TUBERS A HEAD START? PLACE THEM IN OPEN EGG BOXES TO ENCOURAGE SHOOTS.

Focus on SWEET PEAS

If you like sweet peas, but don't want to grow them from seed, buy baby plants, choosing ones with short, stocky growth rather than long trailing stems. Check the label to see whether they're familiar sweet-pea size or compact varieties for hanging baskets. To make them bushier, pinch out in late spring.

GREAT EGG-SPECTATIONS

Who says Easter can't be stylish? Try these easy ideas for unique handmade decorations

WRITE WITH WHITE

Create delicate designs on hard-boiled eggs using a fine-tipped paint pen. With the shells as your blank canvas, experiment with lines, patterns, flowers or swirls for a sophisticated seasonal display.

DECORATE AN EASTER TREE

Yes, they're a growing trend, and it's easy to make and decorate your own to use as a centrepiece on your Easter table. Place a handful of blossom-tree branches, traditionally willow catkins, in a bucket or vase at various heights and hang eggs — chocolate or ornamental — from them with coloured twine or ribbon. ❧

PUT ALL YOUR EGGS
IN ONE VASE

To create this stunning arrangement, you'll need two
vases of the same height but different diameters. The
smaller one (filled with water for the flowers) should fit
inside the larger one, with enough space to layer your
eggs in between. Dye or paint the eggs (hardboiled or
plastic) in different shades of the same colour.

STEP BY STEP

MAKE A SPRING BOUQUET

Anemone

Ranunculus

Tulip

Sweet Pea

Kumquat

Colour match

Combine flowers of different shapes and sizes in one main colour, such as pink, and add a contrasting colour like orange to make the arrangement pop.

Remove leaves

Snip the leaves off the flower stems and trim the bottom inch or two on a diagonal, making sure the stems are all similar lengths.

Arrange

Do this first in your hand, playing with placement, size and stem length. Once you have a good shape, tie with string, place in the vase and fill with water. ❧

EXPERIMENT WITH NATURAL DYES

Mother nature is a great source of colour and you can make your own dyes using a variety of fruit and vegetables. With the exception of blueberries, start with a base of two pints of water with 2tbsp white vinegar that's been brought to a boil, then follow the instructions below. The longer you leave the egg in the dye, the deeper the colour will be.

Turmeric

Add 3tbsp turmeric to the water mixture. Simmer for 30min, let cool, then soak eggs in mixture until they reach desired shade.

Blueberries

Combine 500g frozen blueberries with around half a litre of water. Let it come to room temperature and strain in the dye overnight.

Onion skins

Add 500g brown onion skins to the water mixture. Simmer for 30min, then strain. Soak eggs overnight for the brightest shades.

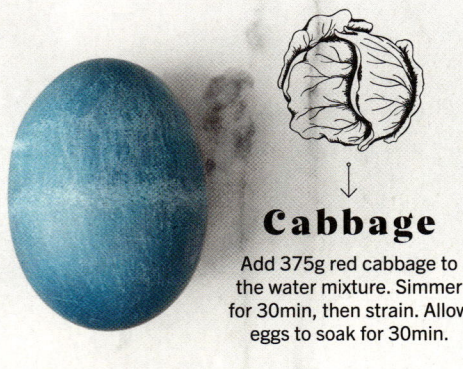

Cabbage

Add 375g red cabbage to the water mixture. Simmer for 30min, then strain. Allow eggs to soak for 30min.

Beetroot

Soak 500g chopped beetroot in the water mixture for 30min. Strain, then allow eggs to sit in the liquid for 30min.

GET STUCK IN

Who said stickers were just for kids? Choose your favourites (see-through ones are best) and apply them carefully to hardboiled white or blue eggs. Think pretty flowers or Easter bunnies and combine them to make unique designs. Slowly unpeel each sticker across the shells, avoiding any air pockets. ■

BEAUTYWISE

Spring is all about a fresh start, so sweep away the beauty cobwebs and polish up your act – fast. Incorporating a few simple tweaks to your beauty regime will make a gratifyingly quick difference, and encourage 'habit stacking' for skin and hair health. Because one good thing really does lead to another.

Spring clean

Cleansing isn't just about sweeping away dirt, pollution and makeup. To get more benefits, choose formulas that target specific concerns, such as blemishes, redness, lines, dullness or sensitivity. Start the day with a gentle cleanser (water-based is a good universal choice) to remove overnight oil. At night, first use a dedicated product to remove eye makeup, then a separate cleanser to suit your skin's needs. Whatever it says on the label, your skin should have the final word. Your complexion should feel soft, comfortable and clean, but never tight or stripped after cleansing.

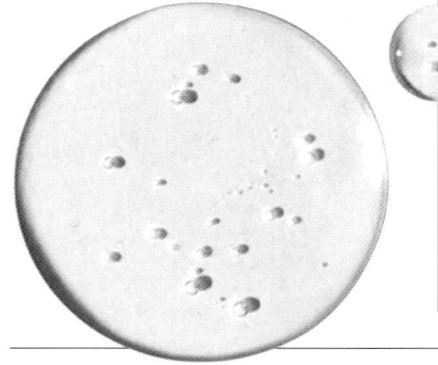

DID YOU KNOW?

MAKEUP BRUSHES NEED REGULAR CLEANING - A MILD SHAMPOO WORKS WELL. LATHER, RINSE UNTIL THE WATER RUNS CLEAR, THEN SQUEEZE THE BRUSH, RESHAPE THE BRISTLES AND LEAVE TO DRY FLAT ON A CLEAN TOWEL.

SPRING MUST-HAVE

Spring has more than its fair share of grey days, so try an at-home glaze to prevent your hair looking flat. Inspired by salon backwash treatments, these glazes are quick to do and easily tailored to your hair wish list. Tinted formulas instantly refresh your colour without regrowth commitment, while clear formulas will wrap your hair in a shiny top-coat to bring your blow-dry to life.

SCRUB UP WELL

Even the best skin creams will fall short if they're locked out by a layer of dead skin, so it's essential to exfoliate regularly. To reap the most rewards, match the exfoliating formula to your skin's own needs. It's about finding that sweet spot – sloughing off dullness without compromising your skin barrier. Resist the temptation to exfoliate more frequently than recommended on the pack, no matter how addictively silky your face feels after doing it.

For optimum results, exfoliate at night to give your skin time to settle, but avoid following it with potentially aggravating actives, such as retinoids. Come morning, protect the fresh surface cells by committing to SPF30+ all year round. It's the best thing you can do for your skin's future wellbeing.

Get to the root of it

Your scalp is the 'bed' for healthy hair, so embrace growing season by giving it extra nourishment. If your scalp becomes dry, tight and congested, it can't do its job properly. A good start is to ensure you're washing enough for your hair type, and doing it properly. Straight or wavy hair thrives on either daily washing or double-shampooing every other day to shift build-up. Textured hair needs washing less often, but cleansing thoroughly is key.

Detox-wise, all hair types can benefit from a good scalp scrub. (If your face is looking dull, assume the skin beyond the hairline could also do with exfoliation!) Then, for hydration and healthier growth, add in skincare-led scalp formulas: your roots will love nutrients such as hyaluronic acid, peptides and niacinamide. Finally, don't forget happier hair is at your fingertips. A short daily DIY scalp massage will really boost blood flow and stimulate growth. ∎

FASHIONWISE

Spring gives us the chance to shake off our dark winter layers and emerge, like newborn lambs, into warmer, prettier, lighter days. Spring/summer fashion ideas from top designers' catwalk shows (usually held the previous September) start to trickle down into high street stores now, giving us all a chance to update our skirt or trouser shape, pick a seasonal colour to perk up neutrals or plan ahead for special events and bank holiday weekends. It's also a time to remind yourself of what you already own and think about new ways to style favourite pieces. Classic spring outerwear includes a trench coat or a water-resistant barn jacket – perfect for protecting you from those pesky April showers.

WARDROBE KNOW-HOW

Take stock of the winter items you won't be wearing again until the end of the year and swap your jumpers and coats for summer dresses and linens. Wash or dry-clean items first and only put them away if they're completely dry. Don't iron clothes you're going to store as this can make the fibres more brittle. Special items can be wrapped in acid-free tissue paper to help provide them with some protection.

That puffer coat? If it's filled with down, so don't squash it into a bag, or it will lose its shape; store it on a padded hanger in a breathable garment bag. Other heavy coats should be placed on hangers together until they're needed again. Clean your heaviest knits, fold, then place them into sealed, breathable fabric storage bags, which will protect them from pests and damp – cedar blocks will also help deter moths. Store your winter boots by placing shoe trees inside them and putting them into a ventilated box or cool dry cupboard.

BUY NOW, WEAR LATER

As strange as it sounds (as winter becomes spring), you should think further ahead and start to invest in your summer wardrobe. Stores release their key buys in spring, so if you need a new swimsuit, a pair of sandals in this year's must-have shape or an occasion dress, now's the time to buy. These are the purchases you definitely don't want to be fashionably late for.

Shapewise

With a trench, you can wear it loose to show off your outfit beneath, or belt it to create a more flattering shape. Burberry's rule? Don't use the buckle. Instead, create a small knot and adjust to your desired tightness.

What makes a good...
SPRING COAT?

Always look out for the following features:

◆ Medium weight
◆ A showerproof outer layer
◆ A button or zip-out lining to allow for weather changes

A great example is the classic trench, which serves as the ideal transition piece between seasons. It's perfectly suited to earthy tones of olive, tan, navy or brown, and normally features deep pockets, shoulder and cuff details, and a belt to cinch in the waist. Pair yours with jeans or pretty dresses and hiking boots.

DID YOU KNOW?
THE DESIGN OF BARBOUR'S BARN JACKETS WAS INSPIRED BY THE WORKWEAR WORN BY FARMERS IN LATE 19TH-CENTURY FRANCE.

HEALTHWISE

Spring brings a welcome boost to our mood and energy levels. We spend more time outside and, once winter is behind us, often feel the urge to move more, too. Both of these mean we synthesise more of the feelgood hormone serotonin, which helps us shake off the winter blues. There's no better time to prioritise nutrition, exercise and sleep to help us ward off health niggles and fully embrace the joys of the season.

FITNESS FOCUS

Hill walking is an excellent way to build your cardiovascular health and general mobility – and it also gets you outside to witness spring unfurl while you reap the benefits of time spent in nature. If you've spent the past few months doing not much at all, start gradually. Increase your daily steps over a couple of weeks, until you're able to walk 60 minutes, three or four times a week, at a decent pace. Then add in hills for a fast boost to your fitness.

Health hack

Plagued by hay fever? Symptoms can occur between March and September, usually peaking between May and July. One recent survey from Allergy UK suggested almost half of adults are affected. Stay a step ahead by starting hay fever medication ahead of the season. Try antihistamine eye drops and nasal spray as a first line of defence, without having to take oral antihistamines. Check pollen counts and plan trips accordingly, wear wraparound sunglasses, shower after coming indoors and shut windows.

IF YOU ONLY DO ONE THING...

Get a good night's sleep! Sleep is known to have a restorative function on brain health – but our ability to get six to eight hours of it can be severely disrupted by the longer days of spring, meaning we sleep less and existing problems are exacerbated. It's easy to let sleep hygiene drift, so following the 10-3-2-1-0 rule can help. Ten hours before bed: no caffeine; three hours before bed: no food or alcohol; two hours before bed: no work; one hour before bed: no screens; and zero: how many times you should hit the snooze button.

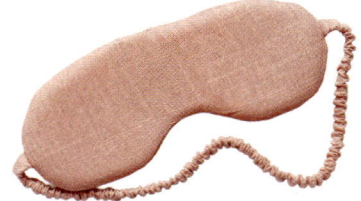

DID YOU KNOW?
COFFEE IS AN UNSUNG HERO. A SOURCE OF SOLUBLE FIBRE, IT'S ALSO RICH IN BIOACTIVE COMPOUNDS THAT STUDIES SUGGEST ARE LINKED TO LONG-TERM HEALTH BENEFITS AND HEALTHIER AGEING.

3 BREAKFASTS TO SPRING-CLEAN YOUR GUT

Flax-berry smoothie

Berries are nutritional powerhouses. Packed with anthocyanins (part of the flavonoid family, known for their antioxidant properties), they offer many health benefits, from sharpening memory to reducing the risk of heart attack. The addition of flaxseeds make this smoothie fibre-rich, too.
TO MAKE IT: To 200g of your favourite frozen berry, add 1 **banana**, 1tbsp **flaxseed** and 250ml mix of **yogurt** and **almond milk**; blend until smooth.

Everything-in overnight oats

Research suggests that people who eat 30 or more plant types per week had the most diverse gut microbiomes (the army of bacteria and other microbes in your digestive tract that play a crucial role in health). As well as fruit and veg, nuts, seeds, pulses and wholegrains are included in the target of 30. This recipe is an easy way to get a head start – full of plants, fibre and gut-nourishing prebiotics.
TO MAKE IT: Mix 40g **rolled oats**, 1tbsp **mixed seeds**, a few **walnuts** and **almonds**, 1 grated **apple**, 1tsp cinnamon with 100ml **milk** and 50g **Greek yogurt** to taste. Put in an airtight container and leave overnight in the fridge; top with chopped **fruit** in the morning.

Mushroom omelette with kimchi

Eggs are rich in protein and pack in a wide range of vitamins and minerals; fermented foods, such as kimchi and sauerkraut, contain probiotics that help feed your good gut bacteria; and mushrooms boost your intake of fibre and potassium.
TO MAKE IT: Fry a handful of **mushrooms** in ½tbsp **olive oil** until soft. Beat 2 **eggs**, tip into the pan, swirling to cover the base, and cook for 3-4 min until the bottom of the omelette is firm. Flip over and cook for 1 min or so. Serve with a dollop of **kimchi**, either home-made or from the chiller section of the supermarket. ∎

NOTEBOOK

TO DO

At home

1
2
3
4
5

In the kitchen

1
2
3
4
5

In the garden

1
2
3
4
5

For myself

1
2
3
4
5

THIS SPRING I'VE BEEN GRATEFUL FOR...

'SPRING IS NATURE'S WAY OF SAYING, "LET'S PARTY"'

Robin Williams

March _____

1ST ___	2ND ___	3RD ___	4TH ___	5TH ___	6TH ___	7TH ___	8TH ___
9TH ___	10TH ___	11TH ___	12TH ___	13TH ___	14TH ___	15TH ___	16TH ___
17TH ___	18TH ___	19TH ___	20TH ___	21ST ___	22ND ___	23RD ___	24TH ___
25TH ___	26TH ___	27TH ___	28TH ___	29TH ___	30TH ___	31ST ___	

April _____

1ST ___	2ND ___	3RD ___	4TH ___	5TH ___	6TH ___	7TH ___	8TH ___
9TH ___	10TH ___	11TH ___	12TH ___	13TH ___	14TH ___	15TH ___	16TH ___
17TH ___	18TH ___	19TH ___	20TH ___	21ST ___	22ND ___	23RD ___	24TH ___
25TH ___	26TH ___	27TH ___	28TH ___	29TH ___	30TH ___		

May _____

1ST ___	2ND ___	3RD ___	4TH ___	5TH ___	6TH ___	7TH ___	8TH ___
9TH ___	10TH ___	11TH ___	12TH ___	13TH ___	14TH ___	15TH ___	16TH ___
17TH ___	18TH ___	19TH ___	20TH ___	21ST ___	22ND ___	23RD ___	24TH ___
25TH ___	26TH ___	27TH ___	28TH ___	29TH ___	30TH ___	31ST ___	

SUMMER

Here comes the sun, and with it the prospect
of holidays, outdoor living and alfresco dining.
Get ready to relax and make the most of it…

Warm days, light evenings and a feeling that the living is easy. Summer is the time we can take a pause from work and worries. To truly unwind, and as the American essayist and poet Ralph Waldo Emerson said: 'Live in the sunshine, swim the sea, drink the wild air'. It's also the season for you to indulge your inner child - the one who still loves to paddle in the water and eat ice cream on the beach.

The spirit of summer is carefree. The kids are off school and excitement levels are high as holidays that have long been in the diary become a reality. Perhaps you're flying to an exotic destination with the family: a place where you can laze by the pool, discover the local cuisine and order a cheeky cocktail, even if it's lunchtime. Or maybe you've planned a staycation to embrace the beauty of the British coast - all 11,000 miles of it. The kind of break that promises salty air, seafood, fairground rides and sand between your toes. ❧

June, July, August – many of the country's most prestigious sporting and social events take place during these summer months. For opera buffs, there's Glyndebourne's flagship festival in East Sussex, where you can watch world-class opera and picnic in the grounds. For artistic types, the Summer Exhibition at London's Royal Academy of Arts is the place to view a vast and diverse array of modern painting, photography and sculpture, with most pieces available to buy. And for music lovers, from Glastonbury Festival at Worthy Farm to the BBC Proms at the Royal Albert Hall, there really is something for everyone.

When it comes to sport, even if you're not an avid year-round fan, there's always something – or someone – to get behind. At Royal Ascot, the hats turn as many heads as the horses, while at Henley's Royal Regatta, the best rowers race along the Thames.

Lord's in London might be 'The Home of Cricket' but it's still played in immaculate whites on many a village green. Then there's the big one... Wimbledon. There's no more evocative sound of summer than the metronomic thwack of a tennis ball going back and

> **'IT'S THE SEASON FOR YOU TO INDULGE YOUR INNER CHILD, PADDLE IN THE WATER AND EAT ICE CREAM ON THE BEACH'**

forth over the net, followed by the roar of the crowd appreciating a point well won.

Gardens are at their glorious best, so take time to visit one or enjoy your own. Admire the architectural spires of brightly coloured delphiniums and hollyhocks as they reach for the sun, study bees foraging in foxgloves and revel in the frothiness of peonies as they unfurl their petals like silk ball dresses.

Our home life takes on a different vibe, too, as summer offers us the chance to move part of our lives outside and treat the garden as another room. Somewhere to sip tea and read a new novel. The place for a casual barbecue with friends (the moment when even non-cooks like to don an apron and rustle up a delicious burger). And the perfect setting for an evening dinner party. Perhaps you'll serve chilled rosé wine, a tagine scattered with herbs and pomegranate seeds, or a simple fresh salad using lettuce pulled from the earth and tomatoes twisted from the vine. Decorate your space with cushions, lanterns and festoon lights and create your very own midsummer night's dream. ∎

PLANNER

Dates to remember

Make a note of any birthdays, celebrations, holidays or appointments you have in the months of June, July and August

Summer goals

1

2

3

4

5

Notes

Did you know?

The practice of changing the clocks was invented by George Vincent Hudson, a New Zealand entomologist, in 1895. The first Brit to suggest it was businessman William Willett (Coldplay singer Chris Martin's great-great-grandfather) in 1907, who claimed we should make the most of brighter mornings by getting up an hour earlier. But we didn't adopt British Summer Time (also known as Daylight Savings) until 1916, after Germany and Austria-Hungary implemented it as a wartime measure. Much of the rest of the world followed during the 1970s as a result of the energy crisis.

SUMMER IN NUMBERS

40.3°C

The UK's highest temperature recorded in Coningsby, Lincolnshire in July 2022.

70,000

tonnes of tomatoes produced by British growers during the summer months.

9

in 10 Brits talk about the weather within a six hour period.

86%

of people claim to enjoy ice cream most in summer with July being the most popular month for the frozen treat.

241.3mm

The average rainfall in the UK during June, July and August.

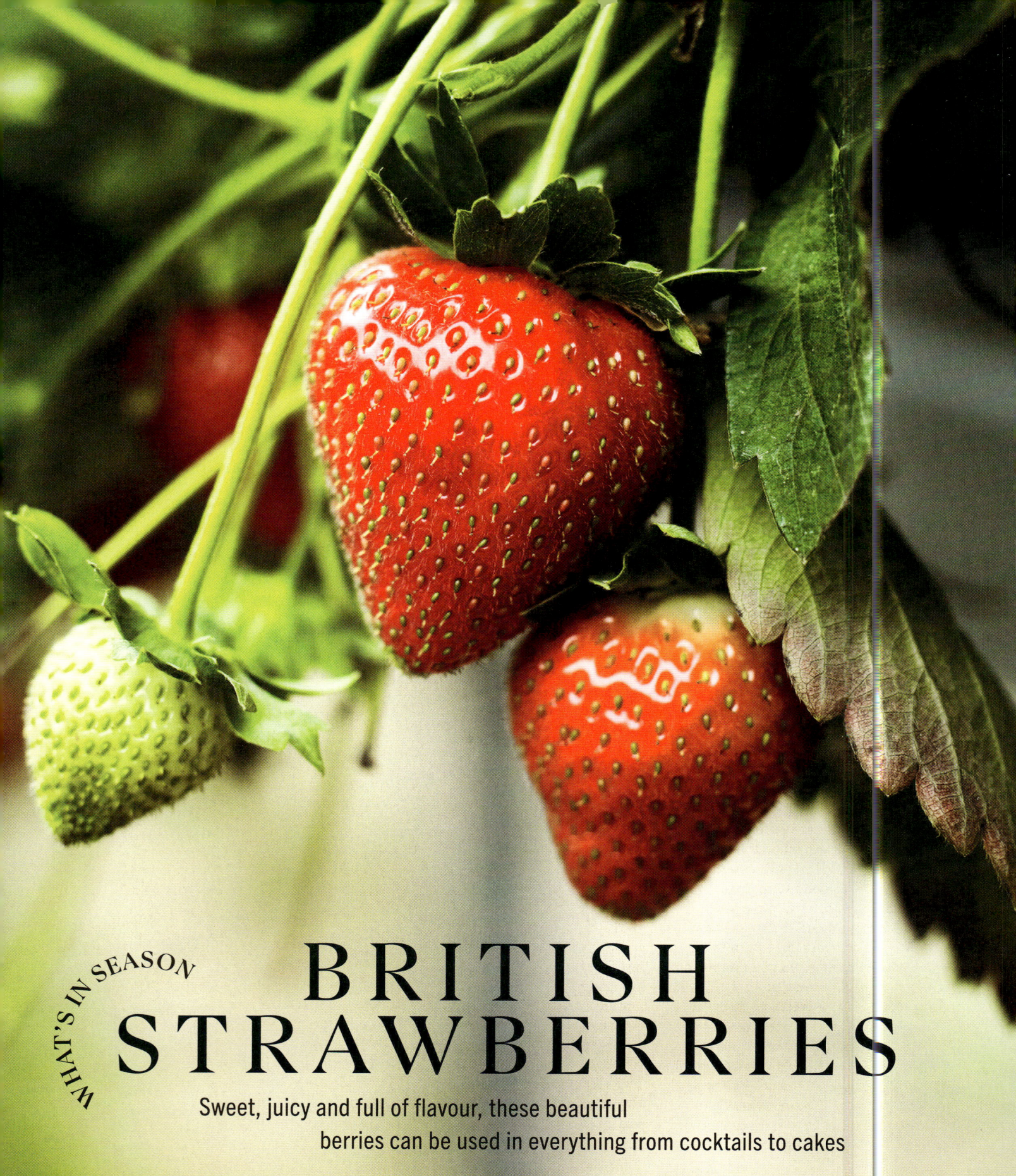

BRITISH STRAWBERRIES

Sweet, juicy and full of flavour, these beautiful
berries can be used in everything from cocktails to cakes

WIMBLEDON'S FINEST

It's no surprise that summer's seasonal highlight is homegrown strawberries – but did you know they're members of the rose family? Or that their green calyxes (or hulls) are edible, too? At their sweetest from late June/early July (when 1.92million are devoured with cream at Wimbledon, a tradition that dates back to when the tournament started), they're packed with essential vitamins, fibre and potassium – eating just seven strawberries will provide you with your recommended daily dose of vitamin C. Head to a pick-your-own farm to fill up a punnet (or two!) and enjoy them just as they are, or try macerating for 30min with white sugar, lemon juice and a drizzle of fruity liqueur to enhance their juiciness. Strawberries are also magical drizzled with a good-quality balsamic vinegar. Look for firm, blemish-free berries with bright green caps – the darker they are, the sweeter the flavour. Store, unwashed, in the fridge for up to four days, letting them come up to room temperature before serving. ➻

STRAWBERRY AND ALMOND GALETTE

This rustic dessert is the perfect way to make the most of summer strawberries. It's layered up with frangipane and fresh berries, then finished with a sticky, jammy glaze – perfect to serve after an alfresco dinner or to bring to a BBQ.

Hands-on time: 30min.
Cooking time: about 40 min.
Serves 8

FOR THE PASTRY
300g plain flour, plus extra to dust
150g unsalted butter, chilled and cubed
50g caster sugar
1 medium egg yolk, plus 1 whole egg beaten, to glaze
2tbsp flaked almonds
FOR THE FILLING
75g unsalted butter, softened
75g caster sugar
1 medium egg yolk
1tsp almond extract
75g ground almonds
Finely grated zest 1 lemon
40g fresh white breadcrumbs
500g strawberries, hulled and thinly sliced
FOR THE GLAZE
2tbsp strawberry jam
Icing sugar, to dust

1. For the pastry, pulse flour and butter in a food processor until mixture resembles breadcrumbs (alternatively, rub butter into flour using your fingertips). Add sugar and 1tsp fine salt and pulse/mix to combine. Add egg yolk and 2tbsp cold water and pulse/mix with a cutlery knife until just clumping together. Tip on to a lightly floured surface and knead to bring together. Shape into a disc, wrap in clingfilm and chill for 30min.
2. Meanwhile make the frangipane. Beat butter and sugar together in a free-standing mixer fitted with a paddle attachment (or using a handheld electric whisk) until pale and creamy. Beat in egg yolk and almond extract. Fold in ground almonds, lemon zest and breadcrumbs. Set aside.
3. Roll out pastry on a lightly floured surface into a rough 35cm circle. Transfer to a baking sheet lined with baking parchment. Spread over the frangipane, leaving a 5cm border around the sides. Arrange strawberry slices over frangipane, then fold in the pastry so it just starts to cover the filling (don't worry if it looks a little rustic). Chill for 30min.
4. Preheat oven to 190ºC (170ºC fan) mark 5. Brush folded pastry with beaten egg and scatter the flaked almonds over the glaze. Bake for 35-40min, or until pastry is deep golden brown.
5. When the galette comes out of the oven, heat jam in a small pan over medium heat until loosened. Brush over the strawberries. Lightly dust pastry with icing sugar and serve warm or at room temperature.
PER SERVING *566cals, 10g protein, 34g fat (16g saturates), 55g carbs (23g total sugars), 4g fibre* ∎

FOODWISE

Summer is always a time of joyous vibrancy in the kitchen – there are oodles of fresh ingredients at our fingertips and most of them require little or no cooking to enjoy them at their best. If you're a fan of growing your own, it's also the time when your garden really kicks into action (weather permitting, of course) and there are few things more gratifying than creating dinner from an assortment of ingredients you've nurtured from seed. Happy eating!

IN SEASON

CHERRIES
The UK cherry season is short, so enjoy homegrown varieties such as Stella, Lapins, Summer Sun and Sweetheart from mid-June to early August when they're juiciest. Rich in health-boosting anthocyanins (potent antioxidants), they're also high in melatonin, a natural hormone that may promote sleep. Eat freshly picked or use in pies, jams and tarts.

COURGETTES
Part of the cucurbit family (along with watermelons and gherkins), courgettes are among the most abundant garden crops to grow, harvesting from July to September. Pick before they swell to marrows and keep the flowers to stuff with cheese and fry in batter (see right).

SWEETCORN
The natural sugars in sweetcorn quickly turn to starch and make kernels tough, which is why cobs are best eaten soon after harvesting, usually between July and September. If cobs over-ripen, dry them out and use the kernels as popcorn.

TOMATOES
Introduced to the UK as ornamental climbers, tomatoes are now among our most popular homegrown crops, providing juicy fruit from July through summer. Always keep tomatoes at room temperature as chilling can dull their flavour and texture.

GOOSEBERRIES
The bright green berries picked in early summer have the tartness they're known for, but later harvests turn golden and taste sweeter. Heavily associated with traditional British puds, they're also great with oily fish or roast pork.

DID YOU KNOW?

ON AVERAGE, EACH BRIT EATS 9,000 FROZEN PEAS A YEAR BUT HIGH SUMMER IS THE BEST TIME TO ENJOY THEM FRESH.

What to cook now

✦ For sweetcorn that really packs a punch, serve it Mexican style, charred on the barbecue then brushed with a mixture of mayo and sour cream. Finish with crumbled feta, chopped coriander, a sprinkle of chilli powder and a squeeze of lime.

✦ For a lovely light lunch or starter, mix ricotta with lemon zest, mint and lots of seasoning and pipe into the centre of courgette flowers. Dip the stuffed flowers in a light batter made with flour, egg and iced water, then fry until golden. Serve drizzled with honey.

✦ For a really easy summer pud, macerate fresh strawberries with sugar, lemon zest and amaretto for 30min until syrupy. Serve the berries over ice cream, scattering with crumbled amaretti biscuits to finish.

3 WAYS TO PROLONG SUMMER

Easy ideas to make the most of your kitchen garden

1
Glut of tomatoes? Halve them and brush with oil and herbs. Slow roast in a low oven at 140°C (120°C fan) mark 1, for 2-3hr until semi-dried. Store in jars with oil.

2
Pickling preserves summer ingredients. Pickled courgettes add tang to a toastie or perk up cold cuts. Simmer slices in white wine vinegar, sugar and spices (try coriander, cumin and fennel seeds) for 3-5min. Cool. Store in jars.

3
Make a cheat's strawberry jam, without pectin, by cooking strawberries down with sugar and lemon juice for around 20min until thick and jammy. The jam will keep in the fridge for a couple of weeks, or freeze for up to 3 months. ∎

GET AHEAD

For the Herby Crust Salmon,
cook up to 1hr ahead and leave
to cool. Make, cover and chill
sauce up to a day ahead.

For the Simple Summer Salad,
cook and drain the beans up to
2hr ahead. Make dressing up to
3 days ahead; chill. Complete
recipe to serve.

SERVING SUNSHINE

Entertain alfresco with easy, stress-free dishes that can be prepped beforehand so you can enjoy them, too

MENU

FOR 6

Rosé Sangria Spritzer

Bruschetta Bar:

Goat's Cheese, Parma Ham and Basil Drizzle

Crab, Fennel and Chilli

Roasted Carrot Hummus

Herby Crust Salmon

Zesty Wild Rice

Simple Summer Salad

Courgette and Ricotta Tarts (Vegetarian)

Boozy Nectarine Pavlova

HERBY CRUST SALMON

Easy, delicious and impressive – a fantastic combination! We're serving this salmon at room temperature, but serve it warm if you prefer.

Hands-on time: 15min.
Cooking time: about 20min.
Serves 6

850g side of salmon, skin on
2tbsp wholegrain mustard
1 slice crusty bread (about 25g), torn into small pieces
50g pine nuts
100g feta, crumbled
Large handful mixed soft herbs, we used parsley, basil and chives, chopped
2tbsp olive oil
FOR THE SAUCE
1tbsp wholegrain mustard
Finely grated zest and juice 1 lemon
3tbsp capers, rinsed
250g tub crème fraîche

1. Preheat oven to 210°C (190°C fan) mark 7. Line a roasting tin (big enough to fit the salmon) with baking parchment. Place the salmon on it, skin-side down. Brush with 1tbsp of the mustard. Cook for 10min.
2. In a bowl, gently mix together the remaining mustard, bread, pine nuts, feta, half the herbs, olive oil and some black pepper. Sprinkle over the salmon once it's been in the oven for 10min (there is a generous amount of topping, so don't worry if any falls off – these bits will get extra crispy). Return to the oven for 5-8min, until the fish is just cooked through and topping is crisp.
3. Meanwhile, mix the sauce ingredients and season. Cover and chill until needed.
4. Transfer the salmon and any crispy crumbs to a platter. Serve with the sauce.
PER SERVING *570cals, 37g protein, 45g fat (18g saturates), 4g carbs (2g total sugars), 1g fibre*

SIMPLE SUMMER SALAD

This makes a great side. If you can't find radicchio, red chicory leaves add a similar flavour.

Hands-on time: 10min. Cooking time: about 5min. Serves 6

200g green beans
1 round head of radicchio, leaves separated and washed
95g bag lamb's lettuce
FOR THE DRESSING
3tbsp olive oil
1tbsp balsamic vinegar
1tsp runny honey

1. Cook the beans in boiling water for 2-3min. Drain and plunge into a bowl of iced water. Drain again and pat dry. In a bowl, mix the dressing ingredients with some seasoning.
2. To serve, toss the beans, radicchio and lamb's lettuce, then drizzle with the dressing.
PER SERVING *77cals, 2g protein, 6g fat (1g saturates), 3g carbs (3g total sugars), 3g fibre* ➤

BRUSCHETTA BAR

This DIY starter is just the ticket when friends come round – guests can help themselves so you can join the party!

FOR THE TOASTS

Cut a loaf of **ciabatta** into 18 x 2.5cm slices. Brush both sides of each slice with **olive oil** and toast on a hot griddle pan for 2min per side, until charred and crisp.

GOAT'S CHEESE, PARMA HAM AND BASIL DRIZZLE

Fry 6 **Parma ham slices** in a hot frying pan for 1-2min per side until crispy and golden. Set aside on kitchen paper. Whizz a large handful of **basil leaves** in a food processor with 4tbsp **olive oil** and a squeeze of **lemon juice**

until it's as smooth as you can get it. Serve 75g **soft goat's cheese**, the crispy Parma ham and basil oil with the toasted ciabatta slices.
PER SERVING *172 cals, 7g protein, 12g fat (4g saturates), 8g carbs (1g total sugars), 1g fibre*

CRAB, FENNEL AND CHILLI

Mix 200g **white crabmeat**, the finely grated zest of 1 **lemon**, 1tbsp **olive oil**, 1 finely diced small **fennel bulb** (keep fennel fronds for garnish), ½-1 deseeded and finely chopped **red chilli** and some seasoning. Cover and chill until needed. Serve with the toasted ciabatta slices.
PER SERVING *109cals, 9g protein, 4g fat (1g saturates), 8g carbs (1g total sugars), 1g fibre*

ROASTED CARROT HUMMUS

Preheat oven to 200°C (180°C fan mark 6. Thinly slice 300g **carrots** and toss on a baking tray with 1tbsp **olive oil** and seasoning. Roast for 35-40min, turning halfway through, until golden. Empty into a food processor and add a 400g tin **chickpeas** (drained and rinsed), 3tbsp **tahini**, 3tbsp **lemon juice**, 3tbsp **olive oil**, 2 **crushed garlic cloves**, 1½tsp **ground cumin** and a splash of water. Whizz until smooth. Check seasoning, adding water to thin or lemon juice to sharpen. Transfer to a bowl, drizzle with extra olive oil and sprinkle on **pumpkin seeds**. Serve with the toasted ciabatta slices.
PER SERVING *232cals, 7g protein, 14g fat (2g saturates), 18g carbs (4g total sugars), 6g fibre*

ROSÉ SANGRIA SPRITZER

This refreshing cocktail is perfect on a warm summer's evening. Mix in 1tbsp caster sugar if you like your cocktails a little sweeter.

In a large jug, mix the juice of 2 **oranges**, 75ml **Grand Marnier** and a 750ml bottle **rosé** wine. Chill. Just before serving, add 500ml **sparkling water** and lots of ice. Garnish with **orange** and **strawberry slices**, **raspberries** and **mint leaves**. Serves 6.
PER SERVING *145cals, 0g protein, 0g fat (0g saturates), 7g carbs (7g total sugars), 0g fibre* ➤➤

GET AHEAD

For the toast, griddle 2hr ahead.

For the Goat's Cheese, Parma Ham and Basil Drizzle, cook the Parma ham up to 2hr ahead. Whizz the basil oil up to 1hr ahead. Complete recipe to serve.

For the Crab, Fennel and Chilli, make up to a day ahead. Cover and chill. Mix well before serving.

For the Roasted Carrot Hummus, make hummus up to 3 days ahead. Cover and chill. Remove from fridge 1hr before serving — you may want to stir through some more oil to loosen. Complete recipe.

For the Rosé Sangria Spritzer, prepare the chilled mixture up to a day ahead. Cover and keep chilled. Complete recipe to serve.

GET AHEAD

For the Courgette and Ricotta Tarts, make up to 6hr ahead. Cool completely in tin. Cover and store at room temperature. Serve at room temperature or warm through (in tins) in an oven preheated to 180°C (160°C fan) mark 4 for 5min.

ZESTY WILD RICE

Using a mixture of basmati and wild rice makes for a really hearty salad.

Hands-on time: 20min, plus soaking and cooling. Cooking time: 20min. Serves 6

250g (9oz) basmati and wild rice mix

200g (7oz) broad beans, fresh or frozen

2 large oranges

1 large cucumber, chopped

50g (2oz) walnut halves, toasted

1. Cover the rice in a bowl with cold water and leave to soak for 30min. Drain and rinse well in a sieve under cold running water.
2. Empty into a pan and add 500ml water. Bring to the boil, cover and simmer for 20min or until the rice is tender and the water has been absorbed. Empty into a serving bowl and set aside to cool.
3. Meanwhile, cover the broad beans with boiling water and leave for 5min. Drain and de-skin, if you like.
4. Using a small serrated knife, slice all the peel and white pith off the oranges. Working one orange at a time, hold them over a bowl and slice between the membranes, cutting out the orange segments (and catching juice in the bowl). Put segments in a separate bowl and squeeze any extra juice from what's left of the orange into the juice bowl. Repeat with remaining orange.
5. Stir 1tbsp salt into the juice bowl (the rice takes a lot of seasoning), then pour into the rice and mix through the broad beans, cucumber and walnuts. Carefully mix through the orange segments. Serve.
PER SERVING *266cals, 8g protein, 7g fat (1g saturates), 41g carbs (6g total sugars), 5g fibre*

GET AHEAD

Make up to a day ahead. Cover and chill. Check again for seasoning and serve at room temperature.

COURGETTE AND RICOTTA TARTS

Impress your guests with these elegant tarts – almost too pretty to cut into.

**Hands-on time: 25min, plus cooling.
Cooking time: 30min.
Serves 2**

2tsp olive oil, plus extra to grease

4 filo pastry sheets

100g ricotta

50ml whole milk

1 large egg

Finely grated zest 1 lemon

3tbsp finely grated vegetarian Parmesan-style cheese

2 large courgettes

1. Preheat oven to 180°C (160°C fan) mark 4. Grease 2 x 10cm (4in) fluted tart tins with a little oil. Trim the filo sheets into 8 23 x 12.5cm (9 x 5in) rectangles. Cover with a damp tea towel so they don't dry out.
2. Working with one filo rectangle at a time, lightly brush with oil and gently press into a tin (there will be overhang). Repeat with remaining filo, using 4 rectangles per tin and laying the sheets at 45° angles to each other, so they don't fully overlap.
3. Beat together the ricotta, milk, egg, lemon zest, vegetarian Parmesan-style cheese and some seasoning. Spoon into the prepared pastry cases.
4. Using a mandolin, slice the courgettes into thin strips. Roll one strip into a tight spiral. Wrap another strip around the outside of the spiral, then keep going until your courgette spiral flower is large enough to mostly fill the tin. Gently sit it into the ricotta mixture. Repeat with remaining courgettes to make another flower. Brush the visible courgettes with a little oil.
5. Cook the tarts for 30min, or until the pastry is golden brown and the ricotta mixture is set (if the courgettes have leaked some moisture, dab it off with kitchen paper). Cool in tins for 5min, before serving warm or at room temperature.
PER SERVING *398cals, 17g protein, 14g fat (6g saturates), 49g carbs (6g total sugars), 4g fibre* ➤➤

BOOZY NECTARINE PAVLOVA

Crisp and gooey meringue, amaretto cream and juicy nectarines – what's not to love?

Hands-on time: 30min, plus cooling. Cooking time: about 1½hr. Serves 8

4 large egg whites
225g (8oz) caster sugar
1tbsp cornflour
1tsp vanilla extract
1tsp lemon juice
FOR THE TOPPING
50g (2oz) caster sugar
Juice ½ lemon
4 ripe nectarines, sliced
3tbsp amaretto
300ml tub double cream
1tbsp vanilla extract
4 amaretti biscuits, crumbled

1. Preheat oven to 130°C (110°C fan) mark ½. Draw a 20.5cm circle on a large piece of baking parchment (use a cake tin base as a guide). Flip paper over and place on a large rimless baking sheet.
2. For the meringue, beat the egg whites in a large bowl with a handheld electric whisk until they hold stiff peaks. Add the sugar, 1 heaped tbsp at a time, whisking back up to stiff peaks after each addition – the mixture should be glossy and stiff.

3. Quickly beat the cornflour, vanilla and lemon juice into the meringue. Stick the baking parchment to the baking sheet with a dab of meringue in each corner. Dollop the meringue into the circle and lightly smooth with a spatula (we pulled the meringue upwards with the spatula to make the pattern on the right). Smooth a depression in the centre of the meringue (for the cream and fruit).
4. Bake for 1¼hr. Without opening the oven door, turn the oven off and leave meringue inside to cool completely (about 4hr).
5. For the topping, heat sugar and lemon juice in a large frying pan until the sugar dissolves. Continue heating, swirling occasionally, until lightly caramelised. Add the nectarine slices and 2tbsp amaretto. Heat through, then remove from heat and leave to cool completely.
6. Just before serving, whip cream, remaining amaretto and vanilla until the cream holds its shape. Transfer the meringue to a cake stand. Spoon on the cream. Using a slotted spoon, lift the peaches out of the syrup and on to the cream. Sprinkle over the biscuits and drizzle with the syrup, then serve.
PER SERVING *406cals, 4g protein, 21g fat (13g saturates), 49g carbs (47g total sugars), 1g fibre* ∎

'MOST SUMMER FRUITS PAIR WELL WITH AMARETTO AND MAKE A DELICIOUS TOPPING FOR THIS PAVLOVA - TRY CHERRIES, RASPBERRIES OR STRAWBERRIES'

GET AHEAD

Make and store cooked meringue and nectarines (in syrup) in airtight containers at room temperature up to a day ahead. Assemble just before serving.

SUMMER AT HOME
OUTDOOR LIVING

Transform your garden, patio or balcony into
an alfresco room and let the sunshine in

GH TIP

Invest in comfy chairs for
lounging and a table for
feasting on sunny days and
balmy nights. Establish
'rooms' by zoning the space
with pots and planters, and
add a string of festoon lights
to create a magical mood
when the sun sets. ❧➤

GH TIP

Natural materials make a room feel warmer and more connected to nature. Try mixing textures to add interest — from the tactility of wood grain to the roughness of rattan, smoothness of leather or softness of wool.

BRING THE OUTSIDE IN

Design that connects people to nature encourages a sense of wellbeing. Make the link in your own home with large picture windows that let the light flood in while simultaneously framing and enhancing the view. Sliding glass doors that open on to a garden will also give a feeling of light and space.

Don't have a vista worth celebrating? Use nature's colour palette of greens and blues inside instead. Art featuring landscapes and seascapes, however abstract, will also give a sense of the outdoors.

Style your home with textiles that reflect nature: botanical and floral designs, but also patterns and shapes – called fractals – that mimic those found in the natural world. Research suggests that these also foster a sense of calm. Examples include the geometric swirls of a seashell and the delicate veining in leaves.

Houseplants are another way to add life (quite literally) to a room, while also helping to improve air quality by absorbing pollutants and releasing oxygen. Choose ones that suit your space – peace lilies and monstera thrive in humid rooms but spider plants or a fiddle-leaf fig need bright but indirect light. Just don't forget to water them! ❧

COLOUR CODE

Green goes well with almost every colour scheme, creating a soothing and serene feel. From darker forest hues to vibrant, zingy limes, use it to transport yourself to the countryside.

BEDROOM SECRETS

Think of the place you sleep as a relaxing haven, and surround yourself with objects and pictures that promote peace and make you feel happy.

A gentle colour palette (soft greens, blues, pinks and creams) is your starting point, as these hues are known to bring a sense of calm to a space.

The bed is, of course, the focal point, so choose one that fits comfortably in the room with space on either side for bedside tables. Add a lamp – low-level lighting at night helps you wind down towards sleep. However, morning light is key to setting the circadian rhythms that make us feel sleepy at the end of the day, so make sure you don't block it out entirely. Opening curtains and blinds will help you wake up naturally.

In summer, layer bedding so you can easily adjust to fluctuating night-time temperatures as heat waves come and go. Cushions add a pretty finishing touch, but not so many that it becomes a chore to remove them at bedtime. Similarly, clutter is the enemy of calm, so make sure your bedroom has good storage, including a laundry basket – don't let those clothes pile up on a chair. ■

HOMEWISE

There's a lightness to summer that's intoxicating and worth reflecting in your home – throw open the windows and move seating around so you can sit in it and face the sunshine. Swap heavy winter textiles for lightweight throws in cooling fabrics and embrace the feel of stone floors and soft rugs under bare feet. Fill rooms with fragrances that evoke sea air or just-mown grass, fire up the BBQ and dine beneath the stars...

SUMMER BUY

However big or small your outdoor space, invest in the best quality weatherproof chairs, loungers and side tables you can afford. And don't forget a pretty parasol to add shade where and when it's needed.

EATING OUT

A casual picnic, BBQ with friends or formal garden party can be elevated by setting and decorating a summer table. Start with a plain tablecloth and patterned plates, or do the reverse, for instant style. Add texture with placemats and napkins, and mix and match wine glasses and tumblers to create a more relaxed vibe. Bud vases are perfect for bringing flowers to the table, or create a centrepiece out of terracotta herb pots or bowls filled with grapes, strawberries and other summer fruits (which you can eat for dessert!). Add height with tapered candles or stylish, portable table lamps or lanterns.

LIGHTEN UP

✦ Nothing says summer like curtains gently wafting in the breeze. Lighten the mood of a room by switching to sheer voile curtains made from cotton, silk or synthetic fibres that help diffuse sunshine.
✦ Put away any rich wool or velvet cushions and throws in dark colours and introduce linen, cotton and silk fabrics in light shades.
✦ Protect pictures and paintings that are at risk of fading in the sun by positioning them in the shade, covering them with a drape or putting them into storage.

Home scents

Look out for breezy coastal notes such as sea spray and seaweed, as well as refreshing bergamot, in room sprays and candles. ∎

TO-DO LIST

Summer is a time to think about fair-weather jobs that require long, dry days – from freshening up your paintwork and cleaning your carpets to washing your duvets and carrying out any home repairs you might have been putting off. These are the household tasks the GHI recommends tackling while the sun is shining.

Time to tidy
BATHROOM CABINETS

Remove your medication and set aside anything that's expired. Packaging can be recycled at home and medication disposed of safely via your local pharmacy; don't just throw it in the bin! Sort through your makeup, too. Look out for the period-after-opening date (an open-pot logo with a number inside); this indicates how many months the product is good to use after opening. After this length of time, the product might not perform as it should and could irritate your skin and cause infections. Once emptied, your makeup can often be recycled at larger health and beauty retailers, such as Boots and Superdrug.

GET ORGANISED
✦ Order your medication by date so the oldest gets used up first. Categorise it by type and store so you can easily read what it is.
✦ If you easily forget when you opened a product, use a label-maker to create a permanent reminder.
✦ Remove any product samples and travel bottles that go unused. Alternatively, bring them out whenever guests come to stay.

Sort your space with
THE FIVE-MINUTE CLEAN ROUTINE

Nobody really wants to clean when it's sunny — but the good news is that just five minutes a day can make a big difference to your chores. Introduced by homes influencer Anna Louisa in her book *The 5 Minute Clean Routine*, the premise is simple: clean for five minutes a day, achieving as much as you can in that time. Louisa developed this routine soon after becoming a mum: 'With a baby to look after, I needed to keep things simple: put away the laundry, fill the dishwasher, wipe the worktops — five-minute tasks that were easy to achieve and made the house look and feel a little bit better. That, in turn, meant I wasn't waking up to chaos the next morning, which put me in a better frame of mind for the day ahead.'

In addressing 'quick wins', you'll feel like you're more in control and a positive mindset will encourage you to keep it up — after all, it's only for five minutes! It's particularly handy in the bathroom, as you can quickly wipe toothpaste from the mirror, collect toilet-roll tubes for recycling and reorganise your towels in five minutes or less. And if you find you want to keep cleaning afterwards, you can! It makes things fun, too — especially if you challenge yourself and set a timer to keep count. This method is more suited to cleaning than decluttering — you don't want to rush decisions about what to keep or throw out, as that can lead to regret and unnecessary stress. ❧

GHI HACK

Summer duvets should be laundered at least once a year, or sweat and grime will start to build up and stain them. It's much easier to do this in summer when the warmer days are ideal for airing and drying them. Always follow the care label, but avoid dry cleaning duvets where possible: you don't want to be breathing in the cleaning chemicals if they're not fully removed (they can be cleaned by a specialist service that doesn't use solvents). If they fit in your machine, many duvets can be washed at home (or in a large launderette machine). Use the highest temperature the care label allows with one-third the usual amount of detergent. With pillows, wash two at once or pad out one with towels, or the weight will become unbalanced and cause the machine to shake and vibrate as it attempts to spin.

UPGRADE YOUR CLEANING PRODUCTS

Buy microfibre cloths, which collect dust and dirt without scratching any surfaces. A squeegee is great for quickly wiping down the shower, but a window vacuum is easier for cleaning windows. For detergents, look for bio formulations that contain enzymes to break down protein-based stains. If you have sensitive skin, use non-bio products. Use a washing bag to reduce fibre shedding and filter out microplastics before they pollute the water.

Clean your grill

Give your barbecue a thorough clean before the hot weather hits. For smaller grills, this can be a simple case of taking it apart while cool and cleaning parts in washing-up liquid and hot water before rinsing, drying and replacing. With larger grills, it's easier to burn off food residue. Turn up the burners to their highest setting, or light the coals and let them get to full temperature before leaving for 15 minutes. Scrape away the dirt, taking care not to burn yourself. Rubbing the cooking surface with half an onion (and a pair of tongs) can also help dislodge burnt-on food.

Life admin

Book the window cleaner in as you're more likely to notice smears when the sun's shining on the glass. After, remove dust from the frames, then spray the inside of the windows with a glass cleaner. You can mix your own cleaner with diluted white vinegar (nine parts water to one part vinegar). Finally, use a microfibre cloth to wipe from top to bottom.

SPRUCE UP YOUR CARPETS

If you can, use a dedicated carpet-cleaning machine. If you don't own one, you can hire them from Rug Doctor. It's recommended you do this once a year, or twice a year if you have allergies or pets. Make sure your carpet is completely dry before you replace any rugs or furniture.

WHAT TO FIX

Painting or repainting is an easy way to upcycle old pieces of furniture or bring a burst of colour to your space, and now's the time to get creative as you can take projects outdoors or open your windows to air fumes. If you're painting bare wood, lightly sand the surface and brush off any dust. For other surfaces, clean with a damp cloth. For a smooth finish, fill any cracks or holes with filler. Check your chosen furniture paint to see if you need to use a primer on your specific surface before you add your colour. ■

SUNSHINE BLOOMS

It's time to stop
and smell the roses
– preferably yours…

In the summer garden, abundance is everything. Take a leaf – or a fragrant rose petal – from the garden of Robin and Libby Ellis, who created this quintessential English country garden at their home in Norfolk. A profusion of planting hits its glorious peak in June; centre stage is the rose in its many forms, from English shrub roses to climbers that clothe the house walls and swarm over arches. All are chosen for their colour and perfume, such as the fruit-scented golden climber Alchymist.

Perennial plants in soft, romantic hues jostle for space: peonies; catmint; perennial wallflower *Erysimum* Bowles's Mauve; anthemis daisies and white foxgloves – all easy-growing cottage garden classics. Dreamy clouds of soft blue are provided by pretty Love-in-a-mist – so easy to bring into the garden forever with a single packet of spring-sown seeds.

The Ellis's garden is a true celebration of summer, but even the smallest of spaces can be made to look glorious at this time of year. Try bringing in a rose or three, and plant catmint or lavender to billow around their bases. It's the secret to an instant sunshine sanctuary. ❧

GH TIP

Clipped evergreens and hedging of yew, *Ilex crenata* and shrubby honeysuckle *Lonicera nitida* help contain ebullient planting while providing structure in the garden in leaner months, when there are fewer plants on show.

MAKING MAGIC

Gardens are a reflection of your personality, just as your home is, so think about how you can add character. Inspired by a trip to India, the Ellises made a feature of a marble statue of Buddha, planting a couple of cranesbill geraniums at its feet to give it a been-there-forever look.

Even the newest gardens can acquire an established feel after just a season or two. Try leaving – or creating – spaces between paving, filling them with a little compost and squeezing in scraps of plants such as *Alchemilla mollis*; Mexican daisy *Erigeron karvinskianus*; thymes; and groundcover spurge *Euphorbia cyparissias*. These will soon colonise, softening hard surfaces and giving a country garden feel, even in town.

Consider, too, having a seating area that isn't by the back door – perhaps at the end of the garden, looking back towards the house, or in a particular corner that is bathed in golden evening light. You could create it simply by laying down membrane on bare soil and topping with a thick layer of gravel, then planting here and there through the membrane to make it look more natural. ❧

GH TIP

For roses to thrive through summer, they need frequent deadheading. To allow adjacent blooms to have their moment, cut off the faded flower at the point where the flower joins the stem.

'NAMED AFTER THE FAMOUS GARDEN DESIGNER AND BRED BY DAVID AUSTIN, GERTRUDE JEKYLL IS ONE OF THE FIRST ENGLISH ROSES TO FLOWER'

FOLLOW YOUR NOSE

Roses that tumble artlessly over a garden wall or fence are an essential part of the magical summer garden, providing vibrant colour and intoxicating fragrance. Featured here is classic Maigold, a musk-scented climber with yellow-apricot blooms, which flowers early in the season and then puts on a smaller show in early autumn.

In the border is The Pilgrim, one of David Austin's English varieties that combine the full-petalled beauty and perfume of antique roses with the more modern qualities of disease resistance and repeat flowering.

FIVE OF OUR FAVOURITE ROSES

Mutabilis

A China rose with fluttery, single flowers that resemble butterflies, ranging in shades from lemon to pink and crimson.

Boscobel

Large upward-facing coral blooms and glossy dark-green leaves make this English rose a good choice for flower displays.

Summer Song

An unusual English shrub rose with cupped blooms of a rich orange, and a scent of tea and ripe bananas.

The King's Rose

Introduced in 2025, The King's Rose is set to be a royal winner: an English shrub rose with distinctive fuchsia pink and white petals, a fine fragrance and heart-shaped leaves.

Tuscany Superb

A vigorous antique shrub rose that thrives in all conditions and produces fragrant, velvety plum flowers with golden stamens. ❧

GH TIP

Clever planting is one way to
add interest to your garden but
there are many others. The
Ellises, for example, used
a weathered sundial to break up
an expanse of lawn, while, in the
same area, a Lutyens-style
bench at the end acts as
a fancy 'full stop'. ■

GARDENWISE

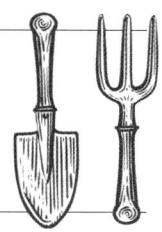

Now's the time to reap the rewards of your hard work – so take a moment to sit back and enjoy your summer garden, as wildlife certainly will be! English roses are at their best in June and July and hanging baskets full of trailing petunias, fuchsias and geraniums will start blooming, too. When it comes to jobs, there's still plenty to do – but it's more about controlling the glorious chaos good weather brings, which means weeding and watering as well as cutting back and deadheading to keep those flowers coming.

Early summer

Dig out any emerging signs of bindweed and brambles before they overrun beds. Continue to stake and support plants before they need it and prep them for drought by spreading a compost of bark chippings around their bases, avoiding stems. Do this when the soil is moist, not dry. Using soft ties or twine, tie in climbing roses and other climbers, training them along horizontal wires or trellis to encourage flowering.

Midsummer

Make more climbers by pinning their long stems into the soil using U-shaped pins. Prune mock orange (*Philadelphus*) after it flowers, cutting a third of the oldest stems to ground level. Cut flowering herbs — thyme, oregano, mint — back hard to promote new growth.

Late summer

Clip evergreen hedges and topiary, first making sure no nesting birds remain. Large-leaved bushes, such as bay, should have whole leaves cut to avoid a sheared finish. When mowing, leave an area of long grass to encourage wildlife. Tidy borders by pulling out faded flowers, dead foliage and weeds to make room for new growth.

NO TIME TO PULL OUT PERENNIAL WEEDS, SUCH AS DANDELIONS? SNIP OFF FLOWERHEADS TO STOP THEM FROM MULTIPLYING.

Top 5: Grow your own

1. Crunchy lunchbox cucumbers grow well outdoors and can be bought as young plants (try the 'La Diva' or 'Mini Munch' varieties). Trail one plant up, over and down a U-cane prodded into the ground or a large, compost-filled pot.
2. Sow peppery mustard greens to add some kick to summer salads: they'll grow best in a shady spot.
3. Make sure cordon tomatoes are well supported by tying them to sturdy canes; boost fruit production by pinching outside shoots and removing the lower, non-fruiting foliage.
4. Look out for pots of bushy basil plants in the supermarket; carefully pull apart clumps and repot each one for more basil. Give the plants a hot spot and they'll thrive.
5. Dwarf French bean plants grow very well in containers. Try the striking, purple-podded 'Amethyst' variety, sowing through the season for a continuous supply of beans.

Be container-savvy

✦ Choose drought-tolerant plants that will thrive through prolonged heat and need less water, such as pelargoniums (bedding geraniums), daisy-flowered osteospermum, *Lantana camara*, lavenders and succulents such as echeverias.
✦ Don't rely on rain to water plants in pots — it runs off foliage, rather than running into compost — and move pots into shade during hot spells.
✦ The pros' way to tell if a plant needs watering: just push your finger into the compost — if it feels dry, it's time to water.
✦ Mulch pots with sharp gravel. It holds in water, deters slugs and snails, prevents compost splashing on to plants and creates a clean finish.
✦ Water plants well if they're in window boxes. These containers' narrow dimensions mean they're susceptible to drying out faster.
✦ Keep a pair of scissors handy for deadheading, ensuring you cut to the base of the stem. ∎

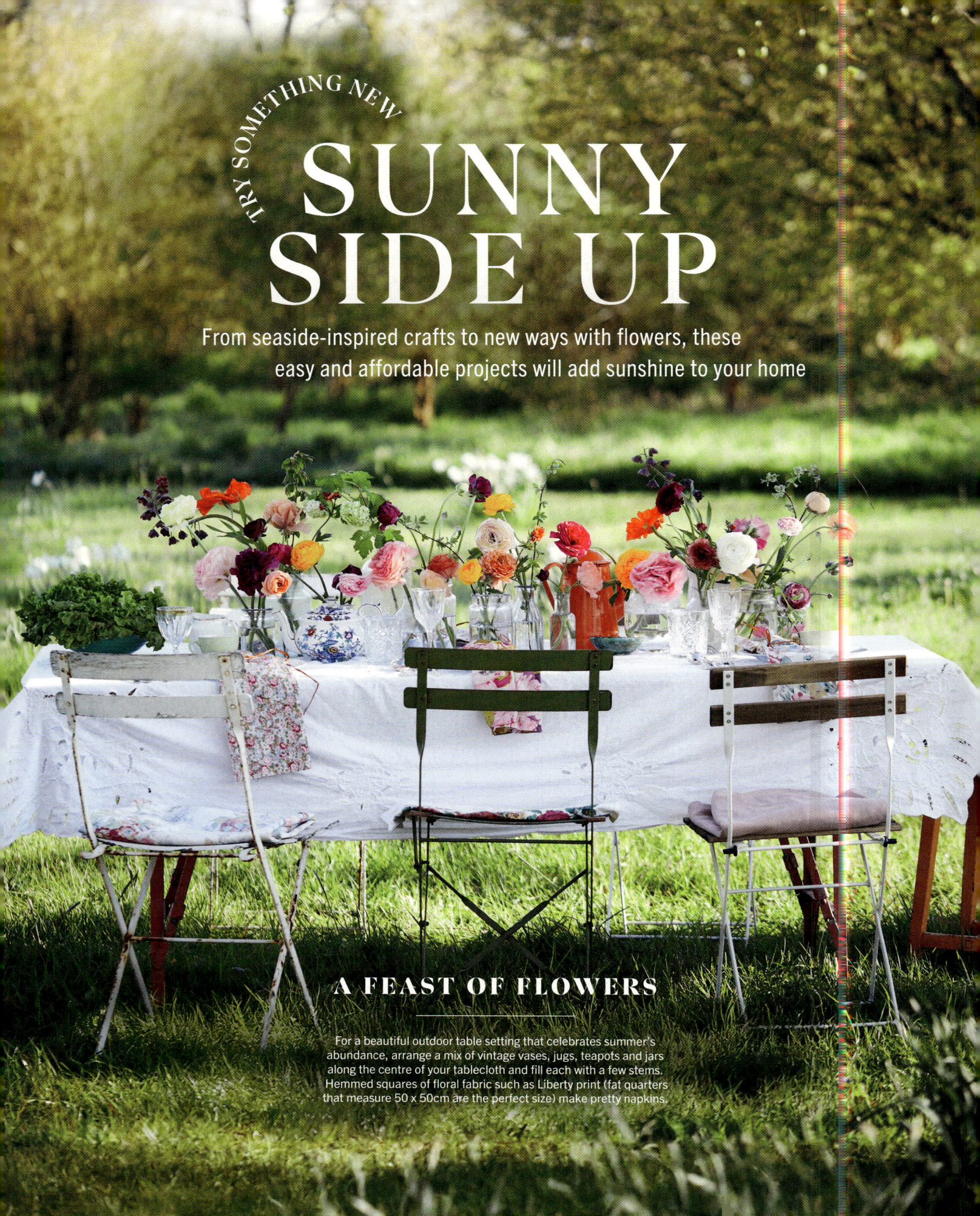

SUNNY SIDE UP

From seaside-inspired crafts to new ways with flowers, these
easy and affordable projects will add sunshine to your home

A FEAST OF FLOWERS

For a beautiful outdoor table setting that celebrates summer's
abundance, arrange a mix of vintage vases, jugs, teapots and jars
along the centre of your tablecloth and fill each with a few stems.
Hemmed squares of floral fabric such as Liberty print (fat quarters
that measure 50 x 50cm are the perfect size) make pretty napkins.

VINTAGE CHARM

Old tea cups make perfect planters for mini succulents. Cover the base of each cup with a layer of pebbles or gravel to help with drainage, then add soil and your plant. Wrap a length of wire around the bottom of the teacup, twist the wire together at the top then make a second loop of wire around the cup to hold its weight and twist again at the top to secure. ➡

LASHINGS OF GINGER SPICE

Make this refreshing cordial by simmering lots of chopped fresh ginger in a simple sugar syrup with a cinnamon stick and a few cardamom pods, until aromatic. Cool, then strain and serve topped up with soda water.

3 OF THE BEST SUMMER DRINKS FLAVOURS

Add these natural ingredients to water or cordials

Mint

Not only looks pretty but adds a cooling tang. Try bruising mint in the glass to release the aromatic oils, as well as serving sprigs on top.

Lime

Whether it's the juice (always freshly squeezed), pared zest or slices in the glass, lime refreshes any drink it's added to.

Ginger

Fresh root ginger (scrub well before adding) adds lingering warmth and spice. Best paired with citrus or other tart fruit flavours such as rhubarb.

BLOOMING GORGEOUS

Have fun with flowers by combining colour and creativity

Pretty petals

Cut petals in a variety of shapes from colourful crepe paper and push green wire (or wire covered in florist's tape) through the centre of each flower, then bend the end of the wire into a ball to secure in place. Wind the stems on to a length of raffia straw ribbon tied around your napkin.

Bottle it

Cut individual flowerheads out of decoupage paper and stick to the outside of vintage glass bottles, using PVA glue mixed with a little water. Leave to dry completely before filling the bottles with water and your favourite blooms.

Let there be light

Thread wicks through wick clips and cut to the height of a glass jelly mould or jar, plus 5cm, then secure the clips to the base using wax. Wrap the ends of the wicks around a pencil and rest on the edge of the mould. Pour in melted wax pellets and dried lavender to 1-2cm under the rim and let set.

Prints charming

Cut botanical prints or pages from a book into the size needed for the back of your shelves, then fix to the back of the unit using strong glue, overlapping the pictures to create a collage effect. ➥

COASTAL CRAFTS

Celebrate a day at the beach with these seaside-inspired ideas

---

Waterside welcome

You'll need roughly 60 oyster shells to create this beautiful wreath. To assemble, drill small holes into each shell, then attach to a 16-inch wire wreath with thin wire until the circle is covered. Use jute rope looped around the top of the wreath to hang.

Pitch perfect

Create a makeshift beach shelter using a length of fabric. Fold in half and cut and hem a small hole 2cm in from each side. To erect, pop a tent pole through each hole and secure with ropes and pegs. Add cushions for a post-picnic nap!

Add some aroma

Dip sprigs of woody herbs, such as rosemary or thyme, into bottles of oil a couple hours before your barbecue. Remove from the oil and use to baste meats and vegetables before discarding.

Candles in the wind

Stand oyster shells in crumpled foil and place a short wick in each, then fill with melted wax beads and leave to set overnight in a cool place.

Personalise a straw beach bag by plaiting bright twine and pinning into whichever word you wish, before hand-sewing it to the front of your beach bag. ∎

BEAUTYWISE

There's nothing like a holiday to focus your mind on what's truly important. We're not just talking about where to go, but also what to take when it comes to beauty products.

Space is always at a premium, particularly if you're only taking hand luggage, meaning everything you pack needs to earn its place.

HAND LUGGAGE FAB FOUR

The only makeup you'll need for a glowing holiday look, day or night

1

Tubing mascara
Technically not waterproof, but because tubing mascara needs warm water *plus* gentle pressure to remove it, it won't come off in the pool or streak if gets too humid. Gently rub wet lashes between your fingertips and it's gone – no need to pack waterproof eye makeup remover!

2

Concealer
Rather than bothering with foundation in the heat, let concealer take the load. Use it strategically – under the eyes, beneath the brow arch, in the inner corner of your eyes – to cheat brighter-looking skin. For a quick eye 'lift' at night, blend it from the outer corner upwards towards the temples.

3

Double-ended eyeshadow stick
For a great multi-tasker, pick a stick that pairs a darker and lighter shade in a complementary palette. Use one alone for a quick daytime wash of colour over your lids or mix the two for a smokey evening look. They're a cinch to finger-blend, and if you pick a shimmer stick, the lighter shade can double as a highlighter.

4

Lip and cheek stain
One bottle with twin benefits, all in a handy, holiday-friendly finish. These won't sweat off in hot weather, the colour is buildable (making them far more versatile than you'd expect), and the fluid texture means they won't highlight dry or chapped areas.

SUMMER MUST-HAVE

Is an SPF, of course! Not all sunscreens are made equal, so make sure it's SPF30+ and a broad-spectrum UVA/B filter. Top it up regularly and always apply it 15 minutes before going in the sun – non-mineral SPFs need time to absorb into the skin to give the protection level stated on the bottle.

DID YOU KNOW?

HAVING A SPECIAL HOLIDAY PERFUME CREATES A 'SCENTED MEMORY' YOU CAN RETURN TO TIME AND TIME AGAIN. BUT NEVER SPRAY YOUR SKIN BEFORE GOING IN THE SUN - IT CAN TRIGGER IRRITATION PHOTOSENSITIVITY OR PATCHY PIGMENTATION.

FASHIONWISE

Ah, summer! Light layers, bright colours and ample opportunities to live our best lives. When it comes to fashion, it's all about knowing your personal summer style. The best occasion dresses aren't inspired by trends, they're informed by the cut that flatters your body shape best. Ditto swimwear, shorts, hats and even T-shirts. Of course, there's always a new shade to try but why not incorporate it with accessories rather than head to toe? And never forget that natural fibres – think cotton, linen, viscose and silk – are your best friends in the heat.

WARDROBE KNOW-HOW

It's time to get your summer wardrobe out. Swap knits, jackets and boots for dresses, T-shirts and strappy sandals – making sure you check their condition before packing them for a holiday.

Refresh white cotton items by adding whitener to the washing machine rather than buying them again new. And check whether your swimwear still has all its stretch and update if necessary.

Shapewise

When choosing shorts, the best advice we've ever been given is to choose a wide-leg opening, as it slims your thighs and elongates legs. You're welcome.

BUY NOW, WEAR NOW

One well-chosen pretty summer top, whether it's a shirt, blouse, T-shirt or light knit will instantly update your favourite everyday trousers, skirts or shorts and help create new outfit combinations. If it's in a light, natural fabric, a summer colour and has splashes of craft detailing, such as macramé, lace, crochet or broderie anglaise, then you have a winner.

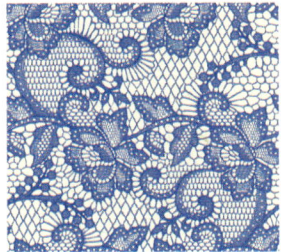

What makes a good...
SUMMER DRESS?

One that makes you feel confident and happy and in a cut that suits your shape and height. The most universally flattering design has fluttery short sleeves, slim at the waist and has a skirt that flares out just enough to accentuate your waistline. Style with sandals and a raffia bag for a relaxed, summery feeling.

DID YOU KNOW?

COTTON SUMMER DRESSES FIRST BECAME POPULAR IN THE 1930S BUT BOOMED IN THE 1940S AND 50S WHEN THEY BECAME A SYMBOL OF POSTWAR FEMININITY.

HEALTHWISE

Say hello to the endless days and blue skies of summer. Prepare to feel your best – getting outside into the sunny, warm weather boosts our energy as well as our mood, and is also great for helping us regulate sleep and appetite... summer really is a low-cost cure-all.

Health hack

Replenish your electrolytes if you exercise in the heat. We all sweat more in the warmer months – and sweat contains electrolytes, which are essential for your body to function efficiently. As well as drinking six to eight glasses of water a day, make sure your diet contains sodium-rich foods such as crackers, foods containing potassium, such as bananas and leafy green veg and almonds, cashews and cruciferous veg for magnesium.

IF YOU ONLY DO ONE THING...

Wear sunglasses. Just as we prioritise wearing SPF, it's crucial to protect your eyes during the summer, even on cloudy days. Sunglasses help prevent long-term damage such as cataracts and macular degeneration, as well as shorter term issues such as photokeratitis, which can cause eyes to become red and swollen due to sun exposure.

3 SUPER SMOOTHIES

Summer berry smoothie

Flavonoids are anti-cancer, antioxidant, anti-inflammatory and antiviral compounds that give fruits and veg their vibrant colour. Summer berries are packed with anthocyanin, a potent flavonoid, which produces red, purple and blue colours. **HOW TO MAKE IT:** Blend 150g frozen **mixed berries** with 200ml **almond or cow's milk** and **half a banana** for extra sweetness.

Cleansing green smoothie

This smoothie is made by whizzing up avocado and apple, which contain a large concentration of flavonoids. Add a small amount of ginger for a further boost. **HOW TO MAKE IT:** Blend half an **avocado**, one **green apple**, and an inch-long piece of **fresh ginger** with 150ml **nut milk**. Add **honey** to taste.

Snickers smoothie

Good-quality cocoa is rich in flavan-3-ols, a type of flavonoids that research suggests may benefit vascular function and lower blood pressure. **HOW TO MAKE IT:** Blend 1tbsp good-quality **cocoa powder** with 2tbsp **peanut butter**, 2 **dates**, 250ml **milk** and a handful of ice cubes.

FITNESS FOCUS

It's hot – and the water beckons. Swimming is a whole-body workout, engaging arms, legs, core and cardiovascular system. It also has a potent impact on arteries – studies show that just three months of swimming reduces arterial stiffness. Gentle on joints, swimming helps regulate breathing, too, so is great for de-stressing. Time to dive in.

DID YOU KNOW?
EATING MORE PLANTS IS LINKED TO BETTER SLEEP AND IMPROVED MOOD; ACCORDING TO RESEARCH, THE MORE FRUIT AND VEG YOU EAT, THE HAPPIER YOU TEND TO BE AND THE DEEPER YOUR QUALITY OF SLEEP. ∎

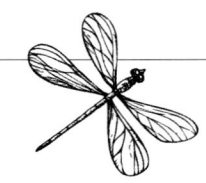

NOTEBOOK

TO DO

At home

1
2
3
4
5

In the kitchen

1
2
3
4
5

In the garden

1
2
3
4
5

For myself

1
2
3
4
5

THIS SUMMER I'VE BEEN GRATEFUL FOR...

'SUMMER AFTERNOON; TO ME THOSE HAVE ALWAYS BEEN THE
TWO MOST BEAUTIFUL WORDS IN THE ENGLISH LANGUAGE'
Henry James

June

1ST	2ND	3RD	4TH	5TH	6TH	7TH	8TH
9TH	10TH	11TH	12TH	13TH	14TH	15TH	16TH
17TH	18TH	19TH	20TH	21ST	22ND	23RD	24TH
25TH	26TH	27TH	28TH	29TH	30TH		

July

1ST	2ND	3RD	4TH	5TH	6TH	7TH	8TH
9TH	10TH	11TH	12TH	13TH	14TH	15TH	16TH
17TH	18TH	19TH	20TH	21ST	22ND	23RD	24TH
25TH	26TH	27TH	28TH	29TH	30TH	31ST	

August

1ST	2ND	3RD	4TH	5TH	6TH	7TH	8TH
9TH	10TH	11TH	12TH	13TH	14TH	15TH	16TH
17TH	18TH	19TH	20TH	21ST	22ND	23RD	24TH
25TH	26TH	27TH	28TH	29TH	30TH	31ST	

AUTUMN

Harvest festivals, bonfires and falling leaves...
make the most of this golden season and its fruitful bounty

The leaves on the trees turn vivid shades of red and gold, apples and pears ripen on the boughs and early morning mists hover over grass beaded with dew. It's autumn in all its seasonal splendour. In the words of American author Lauren DeStefano, this is 'the time when everything bursts with its last beauty, as if nature had been saving up all year for the grand finale'.

Although we're bidding farewell to the freedom of summer, autumn seems like a segue season — a bright buffer zone before the months of winter exert their icy grip. There's still plenty of colour to lift and lighten our mood, especially if we're lucky enough to see some crisp blue skies. And even though the clocks go back and the days shorten (yes to an extra hour in bed!), now that the holidays are over and a new school year begins, we're given another opportunity to make a 'fresh start'. ↝

September, October, November. These months are packed with significant dates. It's when Yom Kippur falls, the most sacred and solemn day of the Jewish year, as well as Diwali, the five-day 'Festival of Lights' celebrated by Hindus, Sikhs and Jains, which symbolises the triumph of light over darkness, good over evil.

And, of course, there's Halloween, once an ancient pagan festival that marked the end of summer, now an excuse to carve pumpkins, wear fancy dress and watch scary movies.

Next up is Bonfire or Guy Fawkes Night, a uniquely British festival to commemorate 1605's Gunpowder Plot. Public fireworks displays and bonfires help us 'Remember, Remember, the Fifth of November' – the date the Houses of Parliament were NOT blown up.

As the weather turns, we start to crave comfort food: think jacket potatoes topped with butter and melting cheese, a spicy bowl of chilli con carne or

'TREAT YOURSELF TO COMFORT FOOD, A MUG OF HOT CHOCOLATE AND A COSY NIGHT IN'

sausages glazed with honey and mustard. For dessert, glossy toffee apples and toasted marshmallows offer a delicious taste of nostalgia.

Autumn is also a brilliant time of year to make jams and chutneys, which capture and preserve the flavours of summer, particularly if you have a glut of apples, plums or green tomatoes on your hands.

You can give your home a hug by tapping into the Danish and Norwegian art of 'hygge' (pronounced hoo-gah), a philosophy we were quick to adopt in the UK. It's all about creating cosiness and conviviality, relaxing with friends and family by the fire, drinking hot chocolate and wrapping up in blankets and snuggly socks. Treat yourself, your family – and the dog – to woollen, cashmere or quilted throws or, better still, learn how to knit one yourself! Enjoy what Keats described as 'the season of mists and mellow fruitfulness'.

PLANNER

Dates to remember

Make a note of any birthdays, holidays, celebrations or appointments you have in the months of September, October and November.

Autumn goals

1
2
3
4
5

Notes

Did you know?

Hollowing out vegetables and carving scary faces into their flesh didn't originate in America but in Ireland. The Celtic people celebrated the festival of Samhain, which many believe is a precursor to Halloween. Samhain marked the end of the harvest season and the beginning of the darker months. The lighting of bonfires was thought to evoke protective powers from the spirit world. Mumming and guising – where people dressed up in costume to visit their neighbours and recited poems in exchange for food – were part of the celebrations.

AUTUMN IN NUMBERS

100

Research has found those born in autumn are more likely to live to this age.

40

The number of years it takes most English oak (*Quercus robur*) to produce acorns.

95

The percentage that the red squirrel population has fallen by in England and Wales in the last 70 years.

174

The weight in stones of the heaviest ever pumpkin recorded in the UK (roughly the weight of a Ford Fiesta!)

20

The distance in metres you need to move a slug to stop it returning 'home' to your garden.

HERITAGE APPLES

They've been grown in British orchards for hundreds of years,
but now some of the lesser-known varieties need our support

SWEET DREAMS

If there's one fruit the UK grows with aplomb, it's apples. Nowadays, apples are largely divided into two categories: cooking and dessert. The former (which includes the iconic Bramley's Seedling) have a sharp, acidic flavour that's more suited, when sweetened, to pies and crumbles. Dessert apples (including Cox's Orange Pippin and Braeburn) are sweeter. Heritage apple varieties, such as Ashmead's Kernel and Cornish Gilliflower, have been grown in Britain for hundreds of years, but have gone out of fashion in more recent times thanks to the supermarkets' demand for uniform produce that's constantly available. The disappearance of more than 80% of our orchards in the last century has negatively impacted biodiversity and wildlife, which is why it's so important we keep these 'forgotten' varieties alive. You can pick up heritage apples at community orchard open days, or at your local farmers' market. The RHS also holds apple-tasting events, a perfect opportunity to try lesser-known varieties. ❧

GH TIP

If you don't have any Calvados (an apple or pear brandy), use rum or regular brandy — or you can leave it out.

APPLE TARTE TATIN

Gloriously golden caramel, tender apples and crisp pastry – this dessert truly is one of France's most superior exports, served here with a sweet, boozy cream.

Hands-on time: 35min, plus cooling. Cooking time: about 50min. Serves 8

FOR THE TARTE TATIN

320g sheet ready-rolled puff pastry

4 large Braeburn apples

1 vanilla pod, optional

100g caster sugar

60g butter, chopped

FOR THE CALVADOS CREAM

250ml double cream

15g icing sugar, sifted

30ml Calvados

1 Line a baking sheet with baking parchment. For the tarte tatin, unroll the pastry and cut out a rough 24-25cm circle, rolling the pastry out a little more first, if needed. Transfer to the lined baking sheet and prick all over with a fork. Chill until needed.

2 Peel, core and quarter the apples. Split the vanilla pod lengthways, if using, keeping the end attached, and put into a rough 24-25cm (at the top) ovenproof frying pan or skillet with the sugar and 50ml water. Heat gently on the hob, stirring until the sugar dissolves. Increase heat to medium-high and cook to a rich amber colour, swirling the pan, rather than stirring.

3 Remove pan/skillet from heat, add the butter and stir to melt (the caramel might look a little split). Arrange the apples in the caramel in one layer, rounded-side down. Return to medium hob heat for 10min or until the caramel has reduced and the apples are tender. Preheat oven to 200°C (180°C fan) mark 6.

4 Lay the pastry over the apples, tucking the edges down into the pan/skillet. Slice a cross into the centre of the pastry to allow steam to escape. Cook in the oven for 20-25min, or until the pastry is deep golden.

5 Carefully remove from oven and leave to cool and rest for 5min (wrap handle in an oven glove to remind you it's hot!). Meanwhile, for the Calvados cream, in a medium bowl, beat all the ingredients until the mixture just holds its shape. Invert the tarte tatin on to a serving plate and serve with the Calvados cream.

PER SERVING *400cals, 2g protein, 30g fat (18g saturates), 28g carbs (21g total sugars), 1g fibre* ■

FOODWISE

As much as it can be hard to say goodbye to long sunny days and eating alfresco, there's always something so comforting about that gradual transition into autumn where warming soups, slow-cooked stews and hearty puds become the norm. We're blessed in the UK with an abundant autumnal harvest, so there's no need for things to get mundane in the kitchen as we draw closer to the end of the year.

IN SEASON

PUMPKINS

There are few vegetables that say 'autumn is here' more succinctly than the pumpkin. These wonderful flame-coloured fruits (they're not actually vegetables) are typically harvested in September and October, but can be stored in a dark place for months afterwards. While scale is everything for Halloween carving, larger pumpkins can have very little taste so look for smaller varieties when it comes to eating. They should feel heavy and sound hollow when tapped on their base.

BLACKBERRIES

Bridging the gap between summer and autumn, these little berries are as at home in a creamy fruit fool as they are in a warming crumble. Blackberries grow in abundance on British hedgerows and are usually ready to be picked from July to September, so keep your eyes peeled for plump, fully purple fruit (and don't forget to bring a tub on country walks!).

PEARS

Synonymous with autumn, pears are picked from late August all the way through until November. As with their apple cousins, there are thousands of pear varieties but the most common in Britain are Concorde, Comice, Conference and Williams. They're easy to grow yourself and compact varieties will thrive just as well in a large container if you don't have a lot of space.

RED CABBAGE

Often overlooked by showier varieties such as savoy and hispi, red cabbage is a really hard-working little brassica, as at home raw in a wintry slaw as it is braised in red wine. Typically harvested between October and March, they keep well for a couple of weeks in a cool dark place, or in the fridge.

DID YOU KNOW?

BEFORE PUMPKINS, TURNIPS AND EVEN BEETROOTS WERE CARVED INTO SPOOKY LANTERNS TO WARD OFF EVIL SPIRITS AT HALLOWEEN.

What to cook now

Now is a great time to make pickles and preserves. Here's our guide to what's what…

✦ Jam is a cooked mixture of fruit and sugar, with the sugar effectively preserving the fruit so it can be kept in a cool place for months without deterioration.

✦ Trickier to make are jellies, made solely with the juice and sugar, with all the pulp extracted. As a rough guide, 450g fruit makes 700g jelly.

✦ Pickles are a traditional way to preserve fruit and vegetables with vinegar, spices and flavourings. Cook fruits before pickling them; if you want a sharp pickle, the vegetables are generally brined first for up to 24 hours.

✦ Chutneys are easy to make, as everything goes into the pan together. Chopped fruit and veg are cooked for hours with vinegar, sugar and spices. The flavour improves with keeping.

3 WAYS TO USE UP AUTUMN GEMS

Quick and easy ideas for a taste of the season

1

For a simple yet indulgent autumnal soup, roast chunks of celeriac until soft and starting to caramelise, then blitz with hot stock and blue cheese until smooth.

2

For a delicious side for a Sunday lunch, roast wedges of red cabbage until the outer edges are just starting to crisp, then dress with a glaze of honey and balsamic vinegar for the final 5 mins of cooking time.

3

Create a lovely berry gin for winter cocktails by putting 300g blackberries in a jar with 2-3 fresh bay leaves and 200g granulated sugar. Pour over a bottle of gin, seal and leave for at least 3 weeks in a dark place. Strain and store the gin in a bottle. ∎

A HARVEST FEAST

Make the most of autumn's bumper crops with
a hearty menu full of seasonal goodness

MENU

❖

FOR 8

Squash, Sage and Chestnut Soup

Beef, Porcini and Ale Pithivier

Braised Garlic Butter Kale

Roasted Mustard Parsnips

Portobello Pithiviers (vegetarian)

Pumpkin Spiced Latte Cheesecake

❖

SQUASH, SAGE AND CHESTNUT SOUP

All hail the versatile butternut squash. Soups make a great starter, as they look elegant and can be made ahead. If you want to make this vegan, simply use a dairy-free cheese alternative.

Hands-on time: 20min.
Cooking time: about 45min.
Serves 8

FOR THE SOUP

1tbsp olive oil
2 onions, roughly chopped
2 garlic cloves, crushed
800g skin-on butternut squash, deseeded and cut into 2.5cm pieces
2 medium carrots, peeled and roughly chopped

180g pouch cooked chestnuts, we used Merchant Gourmet
1.5 litre vegetable stock
2 sage sprigs
TO GARNISH
2tsp olive oil
Few small sage leaves
100g goat's cheese log

1. For the soup, heat the oil in a large pan over low heat and cook the onions for 5min, until softened. Stir in the garlic, butternut squash, carrots and all but about 8 of the chestnuts. Cook for 5min. Pour in the stock and add the sage sprigs and plenty of seasoning.

2. Bring up to the boil and simmer for 20-25min, until the squash is completely tender. Working in batches, whizz until smooth. Check the seasoning and pour into a clean pan.

3. To garnish, heat 1tsp oil in a small frying pan over medium heat. Meanwhile, chop the reserved 8 chestnuts. Fry chestnuts for a few min, until golden and crisp. Set aside on a plate. Add remaining oil and fry small sage leaves, until golden and crisp. Lift on to kitchen paper to drain.

4. To serve, reheat the soup and ladle into 8 soup bowls. Garnish with the fried chestnuts and sage leaves. Crumble over the goat's cheese and sprinkle over some freshly ground black pepper.

PER SERVING *190cals, 6g protein, 7g fat (3g saturates), 23g carbs (13g total sugars), 6g fibre* ❖➔

GET AHEAD

Make soup up to 2 days ahead; cool, cover and chill. Garnishes can be made up to 3hr ahead. Store at room temperature. To serve, reheat soup in a pan until piping hot, check seasoning and complete recipe.

BEEF, PORCINI AND ALE PITHIVIER

Beef cheeks are still a cheap cut, but treat them to long, slow cooking and they transform into a succulent, juicy joy. Perfect for an autumn pie!

Hands-on time: 45min, plus cooling and chilling. Cooking time: about 4hr. Serves 8

FOR THE FILLING
15g dried porcini mushrooms
750g beef cheek, about 2
1tbsp plain flour
1tbsp oil
1 onion, finely chopped
2 medium carrots, peeled and finely chopped
2-3 rosemary sprigs
300ml amber ale
500ml-1 litre beef stock, or enough to cover
FOR THE PITHIVIER
Plain flour, to dust
500g block puff pastry
1 egg, beaten
FOR THE GRAVY
30g plain flour

1. Preheat oven to 150°C (130°C fan) mark 2. For the filling, put the porcini into a heatproof jug and cover with 250ml just-boiled water. Leave to soak for 10min. Using a sharp knife, cut away and discard any visible sinew from the beef cheeks. Dust in the flour and season. Heat the oil in a medium-large casserole or oven-safe pan (that has a lid) over medium-high heat and brown the cheeks well. Remove to a plate.
2. Lower the heat and fry the onion for 5min, scraping the base of the pan to lift up any sticky bits (add a splash of water if it's burning). Add the carrots and rosemary sprigs and fry for a couple of min. Turn up the heat and return the beef and any juices from the plate to the pan. Pour in the ale and bubble for a few min to reduce.
3. Strain in the porcini soaking liquid. Roughly chop the porcini and add to the casserole/pan with plenty of seasoning. Add enough beef stock to cover the cheeks, bring to the boil, then cover and cook in the oven for 2hr 45min-3hr (turning the cheeks halfway if not completely submerged), or until the cheeks are completely tender. Check seasoning of liquid. Set aside to cool completely, then chill for at least 2hr (you want the cooking liquid to turn into a light jelly).
4. Once cool, strain the mixture through a colander into a bowl, so you are left with the meat and vegetables (reserving the jellied cooking liquid, too; you should have about 850ml). Empty the cheeks and vegetables into a bowl. Shred the beef, discarding any tough, gristly bits, and mix back into the vegetables. Discard rosemary sticks.
5. To assemble the pithivier, line a large baking tray with baking parchment. Lightly dust a work surface with flour. Roll out ⅓ of the pastry and trim to a 24cm circle. Transfer to the lined baking tray. Spoon the cooled beef mixture on to the pastry circle and shape into a dome, leaving a 2cm empty border of pastry around the edge, making sure you press the filling down so there are no air pockets. Brush the pastry border with some beaten egg.
6. Roll out the remaining pastry until it's large enough to cover the filling and border. Lay over filling and press firmly on the edges to seal (removing any air bubbles). Trim excess pastry, leaving a 2cm border. Crimp edges and brush all over with more egg. With a small, sharp knife, score curved lines from the centre of the top to the edges of the pastry. Chill for 30min.
7. Preheat oven to 200°C (180°C fan) mark 6. Cut a small steam hole in the centre of the pithivier and cook for 35-45min, or until deep golden. Meanwhile, make the gravy. In a medium pan, gradually whisk the strained cooking liquid into the flour until smooth. Cook over medium heat, whisking constantly, until thickened. Simmer for a few min. Check seasoning.
8. To serve, transfer the pithivier to a serving plate or board. Reheat the gravy, if needed, and serve with the pithivier.
PER SERVING *371cals, 32g protein, 16g fat (8g saturates), 23g carbs (4g total sugars), 3g fibre* ●

GET AHEAD

Prepare to end of step 6 up to a day ahead. Chill strained cooking liquid. Complete recipe to serve, making sure filling is piping hot before serving.

'IF YOU CAN'T GET YOUR HANDS ON BEEF CHEEKS, BOTH SHORT RIBS AND SHIN WOULD WORK EQUALLY WELL IN THIS RECIPE'

GET AHEAD

For the parsnips, prepare to end of step 1 up to 1hr ahead. Cover with foil and set aside at room temperature. Complete recipe to serve.

BRAISED GARLIC BUTTER KALE

A flavoursome way to serve kale.

**Hands-on time: 10min.
Cooking time: about 15min.
Serves 8**

40g butter
2 echalion shallots, sliced into rings
2 garlic cloves, crushed
Few pinches dried chilli flakes, optional
300g chopped kale, woody stalks discarded
200ml vegetable or chicken stock
1-2tbsp chopped roasted hazelnuts

1. Melt the butter in a large pan (that has a lid) over low heat and fry the shallots for a few min, until softening. Add the garlic, chilli flakes, if using, and some seasoning, and fry for 1min.
2. Turn heat to medium, stir in kale and stock. Cover and cook for 5min, tossing occasionally. Remove lid and cook for 5min more, until liquid has evaporated and kale is tender. Check seasoning. Put in a warmed serving bowl, scatter the hazelnuts and serve.
PER SERVING *72cals, 2g protein, 6g fat (3g saturates), 1g carbs (1g total sugars), 2g fibre*

ROASTED MUSTARD PARSNIPS

An easy, no-fuss seasonal side.

Hands-on time: 10min. Cooking time: about 55min. Serves 8

1kg parsnips
2tbsp olive oil
25g butter
1tbsp wholegrain mustard
1tbsp runny honey
Small handful parsley, roughly chopped

1. Preheat oven to 200°C (180°C fan) mark 6. Peel the parsnips and cut into finger-sized lengths, of a roughly equal thickness. Toss in a large roasting tin with the oil, butter, mustard and plenty of seasoning.
2. Cover with foil and roast for 40min. Uncover, turn the parsnips, then roast (uncovered) for 10-15min more, until golden and tender. Empty into a warmed serving dish, scatter over the parsley and serve.
PER SERVING *149cals, 2g protein, 7g fat (2g saturates), 16g carbs (8g total sugars), 6g fibre*

PORTOBELLO PITHIVIERS

These can be made vegan by using a melted dairy-free spread rather than egg to glaze (and use vegan pastry, such as Jus-Rol).

Hands-on time: 30min, plus cooling and chilling. Cooking time: about 55min. Makes 2

2 medium portobello mushrooms, each about 8.5cm across
1tsp olive oil
320g sheet ready-rolled puff pastry
1 egg, beaten
FOR THE STUFFING
1tsp olive oil
1 echalion shallot, finely chopped
1tsp freshly chopped rosemary
60g spinach
15g walnuts, finely chopped

1. Preheat oven to 200°C (180°C fan) mark 6. Put the portobello mushrooms in a small roasting tin, gill-side up. Drizzle over the 1tsp oil and season. Roast for 20min, until almost tender, then flip over and roast for 5min more (this helps with evaporating some of the liquid). Set aside to cool completely.
2. Meanwhile, make the stuffing. Heat oil in a medium frying pan over low heat and fry shallot for 5min, until softened. Add rosemary and fry for 1min. Add spinach and fry, stirring, until wilted and any moisture in the pan has evaporated. Remove from the heat, add walnuts and leave to cool. Check seasoning.
3. To assemble, allow pastry to sit at room temperature for 5min. Line a baking tray with baking parchment. Unroll and stamp out 4 circles, each about 12.5cm – they need to be at least 4cm larger than your mushrooms. Lay 2 circles on the lined tray and top with the mushrooms, gill-side up. Spoon the stuffing on to the mushrooms, mounding it neatly.
4. Brush the pastry border with some beaten egg, then lay on the remaining 2 circles to cover; press firmly on the edges to seal (remove any air bubbles). Trim excess pastry, leaving a 1cm border. Crimp edges and brush all over with more egg. With a small, sharp knife score curved lines from the centre of the top of each pastry to the edges. Chill for 30min.
5. Preheat oven to 200°C (180°C fan) mark 6. Cut a small steam hole in the centre of each. Cook for 25-30min, or until golden and puffed. Serve.
PER PITHIVIER *481cals, 12g protein, 32g fat (17g saturates), 34g carbs, (2g total sugars), 3g fibre* ❧

PUMPKIN SPICED LATTE CHEESECAKE

An autumn coffee order turned into a beautiful baked cheesecake. What's not to love?

Hands-on time: 25min, plus cooling and (overnight) chilling. Cooking time: about 2hr. Serves 8-10

FOR THE BASE
60g unsalted butter, melted, plus extra to grease
200g gingernut biscuits
1½tsp instant coffee granules
FOR THE FILLING
350g full-fat cream cheese
150g caster sugar
425g tin pumpkin purée
225ml soured cream
2tsp vanilla bean paste
1½tsp ground cinnamon
¾tsp ground ginger
½tsp ground nutmeg
3 medium eggs, at room temperature
TO SERVE
200ml double cream
25g icing sugar, sifted
60ml coffee liqueur, we used Tia Maria
Ground coffee or cinnamon, to sprinkle

1. Preheat oven to 180°C (160°C fan) mark 4. Lightly grease a 20.5cm round springform tin and line base and sides with baking parchment. For the base, whizz biscuits and coffee in a food processor, until finely crushed (alternatively, bash in a food bag with a rolling pin). Add melted butter and pulse/mix until combined. Tip into prepared tin, level and press firmly with the back of a spoon. Bake for 15min, then set aside. Turn oven down to 150°C (130°C fan) mark 2.
2. For the filling, using a freestanding mixer fitted with a paddle attachment or a handheld electric whisk and a large bowl, beat the cream cheese until smooth. Add the sugar, pumpkin purée, soured cream, vanilla and spices, and beat again until combined. With the motor running, beat in the eggs, 1 at a time, making sure you scrape down the sides occasionally.
3. Pour cheesecake mixture into the tin and smooth to level. Put on a baking tray (as you might have a little leakage) and bake for 1hr 45min, or until there is only a gentle wobble in the centre when the tin is tapped. Cool completely at room temperature, then chill for a few hr, or ideally overnight.
4. To serve, whip cream, icing sugar and coffee liqueur until mixture just holds its shape. Transfer cheesecake to a cake stand or plate. Spoon on cream. Sprinkle over ground coffee or cinnamon. Serve in slices.
PER SERVING *(if serving 10) 492cals, 7g protein, 33g fat (20g saturates), 39g carbs (29g total sugars), 2g fibre* ■

'TINNED PUMPKIN HAS A MORE DISTINCTIVE FLAVOUR AND SMOOTHER TEXTURE THAN HOME-MADE PURÉE, SO WORKS REALLY WELL IN THIS SILKY CHEESECAKE'

GH TIP

You can keep any leftovers loosely covered in the fridge for up to 3 days.

GH TIP

Mirror the colour of falling leaves and add a mix of textured accessories in burnished gold, deep amber and vibrant orange. Velvet cushions will add a touch of luxury.

TIME TO SNUGGLE UP

Fill your home with rich colours and luxury
fabrics for a warm and cosy autumnal feel

COLOUR CODE

A dusky shade of pink can work as a neutral, adding warmth and colour while teaming well with other hues.

TOUCH-ME TEXTURE

Create a layered look by teaming softer textiles with coarser ones such as bouclé, which appears looped and knotted, yet still feels gentle to the touch – incorporate it in an upholstered chair or pouffe. Woollen throws in looser weaves, paired with tufted and tasselled cushions, add contrast and comfort to any room.

If you can't face wallpapering, try using textured paint to add character or cover flaws and smooth uneven areas. Wood, concrete and metal panels, such as the shingle wall (above) and kitchen splashback (left), are also great for creating interest. But even adding just one or two unique accessories can dramatically change the feel of a room – look for statement lampshades and stands (above). And why hide away your good-looking kitchen utensils? Big, structured chopping boards, rustic ceramic bowls and shiny copper pots and pans can be used to decorate kitchen shelves to great effect (above right). Dried flowers, spiky seed heads and pampas grass look beautiful placed in vases and will last you all season, too. ❧

CHANGING SHADES

Chocolate browns, russets, golds and dusky blues – autumn's wonderful colour palette is perfect for creating warm and comforting spaces. These gorgeous, sumptuous tones are perfect for rooms that don't receive much natural light, adding depth and tone in a way traditional neutrals can't. Team chocolate brown with yellows and reds, as well as a glint of gold. Vivid shades will pop against dark tones, injecting cheery shots of colour as well as lifting heavier browns. Use browns on walls if you're feeling brave enough, or throw a chocolate blanket over a chair and accessorise with cushions in brighter hues. Similarly, a moodier shade of green with warm undertones makes a brilliant base for bold patterns and textures. Blue can be beautifully calming – the duskier and darker the better for a sophisticated mood. Colour drenching is perennially popular and looks great when different shades are extended on to walls, ceiling and floors. Ultimately, the key to this rich autumn look is to be anything but beige. ∎

HOMEWISE

Warm days give way to those with a chill in the air and daily life begins to turn inwards – cups of hot chocolate in front of a crackling fire and slow-cooked stews and soups tempt us to stay in. Make your home a warm retreat by filling it with cosy ambient lighting, sumptuous fabrics and evocative scents.

AUTUMN BUY

Cushions are the homeware equivalent of a lipstick — affordable and easy to change with the seasons. Indulge in luscious colours, graphic patterns and tactile fabrics you just want to hug.

Create a mantel-scape

Decorate your mantelpiece for the season. Start with a silk garland (or two) of green leaves draped across the front, then add in autumn's motifs – faux or real pumpkins and gourds (include ones in green and white for contrast), with a scattering of acorns and pine cones for a forest feel. For height, use a variety of candles – from tea lights in glass holders to tapered candles in gold or brass candlesticks. Spread the decorations across the mantelpiece evenly or load them up at one end, with a pared-back version on the other for balance. No mantelpiece? Make space on a sideboard or shelf instead.

GLOW UP

As the days shorten, ambient lighting is key to a warm and inviting space — create pools of light with table and floor lamps. But don't ditch that statement pendant – just introduce other options to soften overhead lighting for more atmosphere. Look for light bulbs with a Kelvin Scale of 2500K to 3000K. The Kelvin Scale measures colour temperature, and the lower the number (a candle is about 2200, for example), the warmer the light. Portable lights have had a style makeover in recent years so they're not just rechargeable but chic, too — use a couple on a dining table for low-level lighting when entertaining. And always have candles ready (in one of the scents on the right, of course!) for a little flickering romance.

Home scents

Deeper, more woody home fragrances come into their own at this time of year. Seek out notes of cedar, sandalwood and vetiver, as well as warming ginger and amber. ∎

TO-DO LIST

The autumn months are all about prepping for colder weather and enjoying cosy nights indoors. Here's our guide to the essential jobs to tick off your to-do list, whether that's sorting through your book shelf, bleeding radiators or de-bobbling your favourite jumpers. At the GHI, we start reviewing high tog duvets, electric heaters, SAD lamps and heated throws, all worth investing in now to help you keep warm and get through winter.

GHI HACK

A great way to organise junk drawers is to compartmentalise them with boxes, trays or dividers, so everything has its place. Start by taking everything out, throwing away items you don't use or need, cleaning the drawer and storing similar items (such as batteries, ribbons or wrapping paper) together.

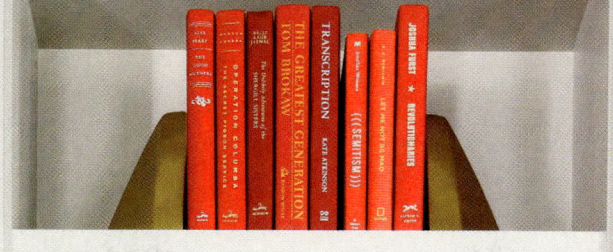

Time to tidy
BOOK SHELVES

Start by removing all the books and categorising them. Create one pile for fiction, another for non-fiction, one for study books and notebooks and one for sentimental books, and so on. Then start sorting through them one category at a time, saving sentimental books for last.

If you're stuck on what to do with a book, ask yourself: When did I last read it? Does it inspire any emotion? Will I likely read it again? Would someone I know want to read it? Such questions can give you a better insight into what the book really means to you. You can then donate, sell or recycle unwanted books.

✦ You can organise books alphabetically, by category or even by height or colour to make your bookcase look more streamlined.

✦ Do not display precious books in direct sunlight, as the UV rays will bleach the spine.

✦ Put heavier, hardback books on the lower shelves. This will keep your bookcase grounded and prevent a free-standing one from tipping over. ❦➤

Declutter with
THE MINIMALISM GAME

The 30-Day Minimalism Game was created by a trio of decluttering experts called The Minimalists; hosts of *The Minimalists Podcast*. The concept is simple — for each day over one month, you declutter a number of items according to the date. So, on the first day of the month, you declutter one item, on the second you declutter two and so on.

It sounds easy enough but things will get trickier towards the end of the month. In fact, if you keep it up, you'll declutter 465 things over 30 days! We've invented a few rules you can add to up the stakes in this game. General rubbish doesn't count and you can't count tiny but plentiful items either, such as toothpicks or hair clips. You also need to make sure the items are physically removed from your home each day, whether by donating, selling or throwing them away.

It's a game because you're not doing this alone; you get friends and family to take part alongside you. The winner is whoever gets the furthest through the month, or you share the victory if you reach the end together. This method is particularly effective if you have a competitive nature. It also takes minimal effort to begin with, which should motivate you to keep going. However, because it's a numbers game, you need to take care not to declutter items you'll later regret, just to reach the target. To avoid this, take your time making decisions and know when to stop if you can't find more clutter.

The kitchen is an ideal space to start. With unused tools taking up space in the cutlery drawer and forgotten mugs littering your cupboards, it's a gold mine of clutter — and as for those glass ramekins.

Clear gutters

Get your gutters cleaned in early autumn before more leaves start to fall, to avoid any water damage to your home. It's also a good opportunity to check for any holes or leaks that can be easily repaired. We suggest calling a professional but you can clean your own if you have a sturdy ladder and someone to hold the ladder steady. Pop on some gloves and clear the debris into a bucket. Flush with water once you're finished.

Check your heating

Bleeding your radiators is a quick way to remove air pockets that cause cold patches and reduce the efficiency of your heating system in winter. You should do this twice a year. Switch off your heating and wait until the radiators are completely cool, then grab a small container and some cloths. Place one cloth and the container on the floor under the 'bleed point valve' and hold the other cloth directly beneath the valve to collect any residual water (the bleed point is a valve that tends to be located on the top-right side of the radiator). Use a radiator key to carefully and gradually turn the bleed point valve anti-clockwise. Air will start to release. Once the air has finished escaping, water will leak, and that's when you turn the key clockwise again to lock it.

Life admin

Book your Christmas food delivery so you can be sure you'll get your turkey on time. Most supermarkets open their Christmas slots in early October – and they go fast – so book early to avoid missing out.

REFRESH YOUR KNITS

Restore your favourite jumpers and cardigans to their best with the help of an electric fabric shaver. For tackling a pile of knits, we recommend an electric shaver that includes a bin to collect lint as you go, making the process fuss-free. Lay your garment flat on a clean surface, hold the fabric taut and pass the shaver lightly over the surface. ∎

GOLDEN SEASON

It's all about colour as leaves turn fiery shades of red, and graceful grasses add drama to borders

As the days get shorter and the temperature drops, many gardens simply fade into insignificance. Make sure yours doesn't by providing a spectacular show of fiery foliage, berries and hips. Even a small plot might find space for a crab apple, such as *Malus* 'Aros', which has deep dark leaves and masses of rich red fruit, or a *Rosa rugosa*, its glossy scarlet hips the size of gobstoppers. A larger garden could accommodate the ultimate 'bonfire' tree: *Cercis* 'Eternal Flame', with stems that each carry a multitude of fiery colours, deepening as autumn goes on.

Grasses come into their own now, developing shades of gold, rust and orange, their silken tassels adding sound and movement. Tall, elegant prairie flowers dominate the borders, while dahlias and salvias in sizzling shades keep on trucking for weeks.

Celebrate this exciting season by replanting summer containers with the colours of autumn – marmalade heucheras, bronze carex grasses, plum pansies – and place the pots where those low, golden rays will light up foliage and flowers, displaying them to perfection. ➥

GH TIP

When leaves colour and fall, make sure you have a balance of evergreens. Be wary of box, which is susceptible to blight. Common privet, *Ligustrum*, makes a fine alternative, clipped into short-stemmed lollipops among the grasses.

COLOURFUL BOUNTY

Plant with an eye to late colour, and the autumn garden will deliver in grand and glorious style.

Heading up the flower display is the flamboyant dahlia in its many forms, from huge, multi-petalled blooms like 1950s swimming caps in look-at-me shades, as exemplified by 'Purple Flame' (above), to elegant single-petalled varieties such as the popular scarlet Bishop of Llandaff. Not only will dahlias light up your container displays for weeks, they make great cut flowers, too. For the best selection, plant tubers in spring, although you can find ready potted dahlias at plant nurseries.

No autumn garden is complete without a show of decorative pumpkins. Two of the easiest – and smallest – varieties to grow from seed sown in late spring are 'Munchkin' and 'Jack Be Little'. And the glistening red berries of our hedgerow guelder rose, *Viburnum opulus*, make it a must-have for a naturalistic garden. If you have just one berrying shrub, though, make it an extraordinary one. *Callicarpa bodinieri* 'Profusion' (right) produces clusters of fabulous metallic violet berries, making it the ultimate star for arrangements indoors. ➥

‘THE LEAVES OF DOGWOOD AND GRAPEVINE
DISPLAY THEIR AUTUMN FINERY’

THE LATE, LATE SHOW

When the summer border fades in August, the prairie plants take up the dance, with swishing grasses that mingle with every kind of daisy flower. Make sure you have your full quota of both – either in the border, if you have space, or as a grouping of pots on the patio, pushed together to look as if they're a small-scale prairie. Our most familiar autumn-flowering daisy is the Michaelmas daisy, the mauve-flowered aster, which becomes something very special in the form of metre-high *Aster x frikartii* 'Mönch', (left). *Helenium* 'Moerheim Beauty', (right) offers distinctive swept-back petals in fiery autumnal shades.

Two more prairie gems are the aptly-named coneflowers, with a novel, central raised brown cone, in the form of deep pink *Echinacea purpurea* and golden *Rudbeckia* 'Goldsturm'. To display all these beauties at their best, contrast autumn's crop of dynamic daisies with the wide, flat heads of achilleas and low-growing pillows of dusty pink sedum *Hylotelephium* 'Herbstfreude', sometimes known as *Sedum* 'Autumn Joy'. ❧

A DRAMATIC FINISH

Fiery shades dominate the autumn garden, but there is a notable exception: the hummingbird salvias, in all their deliciously deep shades of electric blue. Notable not just for those elegant spikes of flowers spinning off blackcurrant stems, but also for its staying power from summer right through to the first frosts, *Salvia* 'Amistad', (above left), is understandably a great favourite of garden designers. Happy in a large pot – the stems reach over one metre – Amistad has huge appeal not just for gardeners but for bees and butterflies, too. A similar salvia that makes an equally great garden plant for the late, great border is *Salvia guaranatica* 'Black and Blue'. In cold areas, give these salvias protection by wrapping in horticultural fleece.

Ornamental grasses add valuable movement to the autumn border. If you're new to grasses, plant a winner such as *Miscanthus* 'Kleine Silberspinne', (right), at intervals through the border, and you'll soon be hooked on the graceful fountains of silvered flowerheads that gently swish and sway in the autumn breeze. ∎

GARDENWISE

Don't put away your garden tools quite yet, because autumn is the best time for planting – the ground is still warm and plants can take root before winter. There's satisfaction to be had, too, in tidying the borders, gathering fallen leaves and cutting down spent flowers. Leave some stems with seedheads, though, for the birds to feed on over winter.

Top 5: Get ahead hacks

1. Give next summer's sweet peas a head start by sowing now, in long root trainers or empty loo rolls, stashed together. Keep them under shelter or in an unheated greenhouse.
2. Hardy geraniums are invaluable for border colour: increase your stock for free by digging them up, pulling sections apart by hand and replanting into bare spots in the border, watering in well.
3. Make leaf mould: rake up fallen leaves, gather them in bin bags, tie, pierce to let in air and leave them for a year or two to rot down. Speed up the process by shredding the leaves first with a lawnmower.
4. Protect bulbs in pots from squirrels with chicken wire, removing when shoots appear.
5. Dig up, dry and store dahlia tubers after the first frost.

Prepare for spring

✦ Plant alliums and narcissi in September/October; delay tulip planting till November.
✦ Whether you're planting bulbs in the ground or a container, add some grit to the planting hole to increase drainage and prevent bulbs from rotting in winter weather.
✦ Layer bulbs in pots for max flower power: Tulips first, on a base of 10cm compost; cover with a 10cm layer of compost; add narcissi bulbs, cover with more compost; repeat, if there's room, with crocus or grape hyacinth, before adding a final layer of compost.

TOP TIPS FOR PICKING TREE FRUIT? APPLES SHOULD RELEASE WITH A SMALL TWIST. PEARS ARE BEST WHEN THEY'RE STILL FIRM.

Last orders for the lawn

Remove thatch and moss with a garden rake. Give the lawn a final mow with blades set high. Where grass is compacted, aerate by making 5cm-deep holes with a garden fork. Boost healthy grass growth before winter with an autumn lawn feed.

The big tidy up

✦ Remove mushy foliage from borders and cut back any faded flower stems.
✦ Dig up self-seeded plants such as pot marigolds and linaria, settling them into border gaps and watering in well.
✦ Deadhead late-flowering perennials, such as dahlias, to keep them blooming.
✦ Mulch shrubs and trees with a 5-10cm layer of garden compost, well-rotted manure or soil conditioner after rain – worms will help pull it down into the ground.

3 AUTUMN PLANTING IDEAS

1 An evergreen jasmine

Trachelospermum jasminoides is the climber with it all going on: evergreen, a mass of white flowers in summer, jasmine perfume and autumn leaf tints.

2 A mini-hedgerow

These berrying and fruiting shrubs, planted cheek by jowl, make a great wildlife hotel: *Rosa rugosa*, hawthorn, *Viburnum opulus* 'Compactum' and crab apple.

3 A winter-flowering shrub

Plant *Viburnum tinus* or scented witch hazel near the house or by a path to help brighten grey days. ■

TRY SOMETHING NEW

CREEPY CRAFTING

Upgrade your Halloween decorations with these spooky yet stylish ideas for carving pumpkins, making wreaths and arranging autumn flowers

RELIGHT MY FIRE

For this dramatic fireplace display, cut an opening at the *bottom* of each pumpkin (this helps them keep their structure) and scoop out the innards. Once you've carved the flames, make your pumpkins last longer by spraying them with a water and vinegar solution.

FALLING LEAVES

Not all pumpkins have to be carved! Try painting them a different colour and decorating the outside with pretty autumn leaf shapes. Trace leaves on to red, orange and yellow tissue paper, cut out and decoupage on to the surface using a thin layer of spray-on glue with varnish to seal. To add veins, push the paper with a flat-head brush. ❧

RISE AND SHINE

Another great way to use up pumpkins is to turn them into quirky vases. Carve out the middle, slide in and secure a plastic cup filled with water for flowers and paint or decorate the outside — rose gold works beautifully.

HOW TO CREATE AN AUTUMN DISPLAY

Add drama to Halloween flowers with these three top tips

Use pretty petals

Choose flowers with spiky or unusually shaped petals, such as dahlias, to add interest and colour.

Add greenery

Trailing greenery, such as ivy, adds colour, texture and shape to a display. Use it to create the outline you want and to balance upright blooms.

Try dark colours

Looks for roses in deep, velvety reds to give your arrangement a blood-stained, spooky feel.

ON THE EDGE

Who says pumpkins are just for Halloween? Create an autumnal display for shelves or sideboards by carving them with scalloped edges and turning smaller gourds into natural bud vases. ➥

A WARM WELCOME

Four ideas for autumn wreaths that will brighten your front door

Potty for pots

Thread small terracotta pots on to floral wire through their drainage holes, then on to a wire wreath. Finish with a pretty bow.

Pining for you

Wrap a wire wreath with hessian ribbon. Paint the tips of similar-sized pine cones in different hues of acrylic paint. Attach cones with wire.

Farm chic

A rustic sieve or tray will make a unique wreath. Glue an area with flower foam and stick in flowers and grasses; glue on nuts and berries to finish.

Get corny

Detach the husks from one side each of 20 decorative corn ears. Hot glue the corns to their husks, then to an 18-inch wire wreath.

TOP CARVING TIPS

Pumpkin tricks that will give you a treat when your creations last beyond Halloween

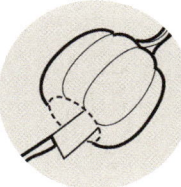

START AT THE BOTTOM
Make your hole underneath the pumpkin instead of on top. That way you can just place it over the light source and avoid getting your arms messy.

SCRAPE THE WALLS
When hollowing, use a metal spoon or ice cream scoop to remove as much pulp as possible. Any strands or goop that's left behind will speed up the rotting process.

KEEP IT SHINY
To avoid shrivelled pumpkins on your doorstep, spread a thin layer of petroleum jelly along the raw edges immediately after carving to create a moisture barrier. ∎

Dot to dot

Map out your pattern with permanent marker on a hollowed-out pumpkin. Leave room between dots so the structure of the pumpkin stays solid. To add the holes, use a power drill and two drill bits of different sizes, or gently hammer copper tubes through the surface so they work like cookie cutters.

BEAUTYWISE

If summer is the time to lie back and relax, autumn is the season to lean back in – and that goes for your beauty regime, too. Your skin's needs change as the temperature falls, meaning this is the ideal moment to assess your daily routine and consider how to put your best face forward. The secret to this seasonal recalibration? Keep things simple. Look beyond the hype and marketing noise, and base your autumn regime on these five proven ingredients loved by beauty editors and dermatologists alike.

5 skin-friendly ingredients for an autumn reset

1

Retinoids

Why: The gold standard of time-defying skincare. There's a whole family of these vitamin A derivatives that are proven to speed up cell turnover and switch on collagen production. **Tip:** Consider retinal over its sibling, retinol – it's better tolerated but just as effective.

2

Hyaluronic acid

Why: The instant skin plumper. Hyaluronic acid (HA) binds to water and locks it into the dermis, keeping skin fresh, hydrated and smooth. **Tip:** Look for formulas with different weights of HA, which work at different dermal depths.

3

Peptides

Why: The messenger molecules that regulate and regenerate your skin. They tell your cells to perform tasks such as building more elastin and collagen or reducing inflammation. **Tip:** Look for products that contain lipids as well – these oil-like molecules can enhance peptides' effectiveness.

4

Vitamin C

Why: The brightener that's never been bettered. A true multi-tasker, vitamin C acts as a damage-preventing antioxidant, pigmentation fader and potent collagen booster. **Tip:** It's traditionally a fragile ingredient, so look for a modern format that keeps it stabilised.

5

Niacinamide

Why: The does-it-all superstar of the skincare world. As well as quelling free radical damage, it regulates oil production, minimises pores, boosts the skin barrier, reduces redness, soothes sensitivity and can smooth wrinkles. Crucially, it also tends to play nicely with practically every other skincare ingredient. **Tip:** To get the full benefits of niacinamide, look for an active concentration around the 5% mark.

Head to toe

Don't stop at your neck. Rather than putting body care into hibernation mode, this is an excellent opportunity to slather nourishing cream everywhere as the weather cools. Active ingredients that are normally associated with facial skincare will also make all the difference to skin elsewhere; ceramides and botanical oils are particularly effective if you're prone to dryness. Make it a mindful daily moment to pause and breathe as you give your body the care it deserves. You'll be thankful once spring arrives.

DID YOU KNOW?

YOU NEED AT LEAST FOUR WEEKS TO START SEEING THE EFFECTS OF A SKIN CREAM OR SERUM – YOUR SKIN'S CELLS TAKE THAT LONG TO TURN OVER.

AUTUMN MUST-HAVE

Bring your hair back to life after a long, hot summer by swapping your regular conditioner for a treatment mask, using it after every wash for at least a month. Even if you don't have time to leave it in for as long as directed every time, the more intensive ingredients will deliver visible benefits ■

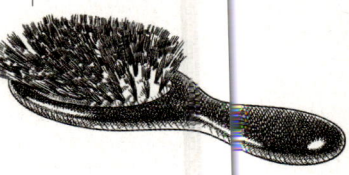

FASHIONWISE

September always brings that back-to-school feeling, and with it the chance to start again and experiment with the new season's fashion trends. The changing weather means layering becomes your best friend and every outfit is a chance to experiment with texture, pattern and colour, whether you're pulling on boots, reaching for a silk square scarf or adding a bold knit.

Shapewise

Ankle boots that hit just above the ankle help to elongate the appearance of your legs, especially when worn with darker tights or slim jeans. A small block heel gives extra polish, but flats can look just as chic – it's all in the styling.

WARDROBE KNOW-HOW

Pack away your most summery pieces – those strappy dresses and beachy sandals won't be needed for a while – and bring forward layering staples, including long-sleeved tops, silk knits and go-with-everything jackets. Lighter dresses can stay out if you plan to pair them with jumpers and tights – the fastest way to reinvent your summer favourites.

What makes a good...
PAIR OF AUTUMN BOOTS?

These are your everyday heroes, so they should be hardwearing and as well made as possible. Look for:

✦ A weatherproof upper (leather or good-quality vegan alternatives)
✦ Thick, grippy soles for slippery pavements
✦ A warm lining (or room for cosy socks)
✦ Easy on-and-off fastenings (zips or elasticated panels)
✦ A shape that works with both trousers and dresses

Choose wisely, and you'll wonder how you got through autumn without them.

DID YOU KNOW?

THE CHELSEA BOOT WAS DESIGNED BY QUEEN VICTORIA'S SHOEMAKER, J. SPARKES-HALL. THE ELASTICATED SIDES WERE DESIGNED SO SHE COULD WALK AND HORSE RIDE COMFORTABLY.

Buy now, wear later

Invest in a mood-enhancing jumper. Choose one with a statement pop of colour or bold pattern, and pair it with midi skirts, jeans and lighter dresses. For a more formal look, opt for fine knits in neutral colours that fit well, or for a relaxed weekend vibe, go for chunkier knits over a casual shirt. ∎

HEALTHWISE

September is here, and with it comes autumn's diminishing daylight and cooler temperatures. Eating seasonal fruit and vegetables, rich in micronutrients, will help prep our bodies for the darker days of winter ahead, as will taking more supplements – starting with vitamin D. For now, make the most of the warmth by getting outdoors when you can; this will help reset your body clock. Resist the urge to hibernate; socialising with friends and family can prevent a seasonal slump and boost your mood.

Fitness focus

Your body has a natural tendency to store fat over winter. Do the groundwork now and help keep yourself in shape with gentle fitness-boosting cardio work – try going on longer cycle rides, walks or runs. Autumn is a particularly good time to enjoy this sort of exercise; take advantage of the last of the longer days before winter's dark evenings set in.

Health hack

Focus on 'social wellness'. Research shows that strong bonds with friends and family keep us well. It's tempting to hibernate once the evenings draw in, but make sure to keep your social circle close – reply to messages, dedicate time to phone calls and use this journal or set an alert on your phone to remember birthdays, graduations and important events even if you don't feel like going out. A review of 38 studies found that friendships significantly scaffold wellbeing and can protect against mental health issues such as depression and anxiety.

IF YOU ONLY DO ONE THING...

Scientists are only beginning to understand the full impact that low vitamin D levels have on our health, but evidence shows that vitamin D is good for our bone health, muscle function and immunity. The NHS recommends we consider taking a 10mcg supplement from October to March, as this is when the sun is not as strong. Certain groups should take this year round, such as over 65s, anyone housebound, those who cover up for cultural reasons and people with darker skin. Vitamin D3 is recommended over D2, as it tends to raise blood levels of vitamin D higher and or longer.

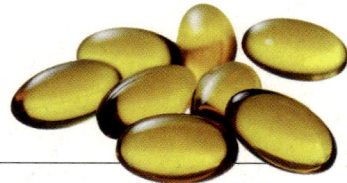

3 IMMUNITY-BOOSTING SOUPS

Roasted root vegetable and garlic soup

Root vegetables are low in calories and high in immunity-boosting antioxidants. Studies suggest allicin, a compound found in garlic and several other alliums, is antimicrobial and antioxidant, and has been linked to benefits for cardiovascular health, and even cancer prevention.
TO MAKE IT: Roast 2-3 cloves of **garlic**, ½ chopped **butternut squash**, 2 chopped **parsnips**, and 2 chopped **carrots** for 30min. Squeeze the garlic cloves out of their skins, add to the chopped veg then put everything into a pan, add 500ml hot **vegetable stock**, season and blend. Serve with a spoonful of **yogurt** and scatter with **sunflower seeds** and fresh **sage**.

Carrot and ginger soup

This warming soup contains ginger, which has powerful anti-inflammatory and antioxidant properties, and carrots, which are rich in health-supporting beta-carotene.
TO MAKE IT: Fry 1 chopped **onion** in 1tbsp **olive oil** for a few min. Add 1 crushed clove of **garlic**, 1tbsp grated **ginger** and 6 chopped **carrots** and sauté for a further 2min. Add 400ml tin **coconut milk** and 500ml hot **vegetable stock**, then simmer gently for 20min. Blend, season and serve with an extra swirl of **coconut milk**.

Lentil and turmeric soup

Protein-packed lentils contain iron, essential for producing red blood cells and avoiding anaemia, while turmeric has protective compounds, including curcumin, that may help combat inflammation. Lemons add vitamin C, essential for immune system function. They also contain flavonoids for an anti-inflammatory effect. Serve with black pepper, which enhances the absorption of curcumin.
TO MAKE IT: Fry 1 chopped **red onion**, 1 chopped **celery stick** and 1 chopped **carrot** with 1tsp **turmeric** in 1tbsp **olive oil**; add 400g tin **tomatoes**, 300g **dried red lentils** and 1½l **stock**. Simmer gently for 20min, season, add juice and zest of 1 **lemon** and blend. ■

DID YOU KNOW?
GETTING OUT OF BED EARLIER FOR A WALK TO INCREASE YOUR EXPOSURE TO DAYLIGHT IS THE BEST WAY TO RESET YOUR BODY CLOCK AND PREVENT SLUMPS LATER IN THE DAY.

The winter garden has many joys: the silvered beauty of morning frost on seedheads; bright white snow tipping stems and branches; the first snowdrops scattered on the grass; mats of soft pink and white cyclamen beneath the trees.

There are many plants that flourish in the coldest weather, so make sure your garden has its fair share. Some of the finest are shrubs that deliver delicious perfume, which will enhance your outdoor space, however chilly. Give yourself views that lift light levels as well as your spirits, perhaps the citrus stems of a yellow dogwood near the house, or pale-flowered clematis 'Wisley Cream' beyond the kitchen window. On the patio, embrace the frost with container displays that will shine out on grey days and in fading light.

Beneath the potfuls of white violas, pansies and ivy trails, bury bulbs of early-flowering white narcissi, such as 'Thalia', for a spring hurrah. ❦➤

66

'THE WAXY, BUTTER-YELLOW FLOWERS
OF WINTERSWEET STUD THE BARE BRANCHES
FROM JANUARY'

SCENTS AND SENSIBILITY

Give yourself a good reason to be led up the garden path by planting a fragrant, winter-flowering shrub at the far end of the garden. The spicy scents of exotic witch hazel *Hamamelis* (right) are worth the trek, and those showy blooms sprouting from bare twigs resemble exotic chenille spiders.

Plant something deliciously perfumed by the patio. Christmas box, *Sarcococca confusa* (above), forms a compact evergreen dome that, from late winter, is covered with sprays of tufted white flowers. You don't need to bend down to smell the luscious honey scent, because it's carried on the air.

Just a few twigs of wintersweet, *Chimonanthes praecox* (left), in a display, will scent a room with spicy lemon fragrance. The waxy, butter-yellow flowers stud the bare branches from January.

Honeysuckle's reputation for great scent is upheld with the winter version, shrubby honeysuckle *Lonicera x purpusii*. 'Winter Beauty' is the garden-friendly version; its sweetly perfumed clusters of creamy flowers on bare branches can be clipped to give you jugfuls of fragrant garden flower stems – better than any scented candle. ❧

WINTER BRIGHTS

Liven up the garden at this time of year with one or two brightly coloured shrubs, climbers or container plants. *Viburnum x bodnantense* 'Dawn' (above right), for instance, has, on bare stems, pretty clusters of sugar-pink flowers that are fragrant, too.

You could clothe a doorway, a bare, sunny wall or even the garden shed with an evergreen climber that has glossy green leaves that bronze in winter and produce masses of creamy bell flowers until spring. As a bonus, easy-growing *Clematis cirrhosa* 'Wisley Cream' needs no pruning, and bees will love the late nectar source.

Holly is the traditional, much-loved winter berry, but closer to the ground, *Iris foetidissima* (above left), displays rows of vibrant orange seeds the size of peas when the seed pods split. This native iris will usefully thrive in shade beneath trees, which is the best place, too, for the perennial Christmas rose, *Helleborus niger* (right). Those brave flowers will push up through snow every January, and make the best cut flower for indoors, reminding us that even in the coldest weather there are delights to be had in the winter garden. ■

GARDENWISE

It's time to tidy up outdoors, clear paths, lawns and gutters of mushy leaves, clean your pots, sharpen your secateurs and wipe down the spade. It'll be spring before you know it, so enjoy the rest!

Winter planting

✦ Plant up containers for the patio to bring in elements of warming colour. Red-berried skimmia, pansies, primulas and pink-berried gaultheria are all good choices.

✦ Plant snowdrops 'in the green' as plants rather than bulbs.

✦ Plant out bare-root fruit trees and bushes, as well as roses, while dormant.

✦ Transplant self-seeded foxgloves that have sprung up in the wrong spot, replanting them and then watering them in well.

PLOT AND PLAN

Leaf through plant catalogues to see what to grow and sow in your garden next year. For the best selections, get your orders in before spring. Consider a potful of dazzling 'Stargazer' lilies for next summer, just from a trio of bulbs pushed into compost come spring. Or how about a mini meadow of golden California poppies, scattered on the ground from a handful of seed? Plan your kitchen garden and think about growing fruit and veg that are harder to find in the shops, such as chestnut-flavoured 'Pink Fir Apple' potatoes or Japanese mustard leaves, to spice up your salads.

Don't forget the wildlife!

1 Put out high-fat food for birds and add bird boxes around the garden.

2 Leave stems of seedheads and berries to provide pit-stop snacks for birds and insects.

3 A float or football will prevent ponds from freezing over, creating a hole for wildlife.

4 Supply birds with a fresh source of water every day. ■

FOR MORE ROSES, CUT PENCIL-THICK STEMS A FOOT LONG AND PUSH, RIGHT WAY UP, INTO A DEEP POT OF COMPOST. ONE YEAR ON, YOU CAN PLANT THEM.

CLEAR, CLEAN, CUT BACK

1. Cut back wayward stems of roses, buddleias and lavatera to prevent wind loosening shrubs' roots.
2. Prune shrub roses, cutting out any damaged or crossing stems to improve air flow. Remove all foliage on the shrubs or around their bases, to avoid chances of future disease.
3. Cut down any dead stems and foliage on perennials.
4. Prune side shoots on wisteria back to a couple of buds for more flowers.
5. Prune apple and pear trees, removing any crowded and crossing shoots at the centre, for more fruits next year.
6. Knock off any snow that settles on branches, potentially damaging them, with a broom or bamboo cane.

Protect and prevent

✦ Terracotta pots aren't always frostproof. Scrub, dry and store those that are empty, and protect containers – and the plants' roots – with a layer of bubblewrap.

✦ Wrap two layers of horticultural fleece around borderline hardy plants, securing with string or staples or, more easily, buy large fleece drawstring bags to pull over plants. For plants with foliage fans, gather leaves vertically first and tie together – it's the central growing point that's vulnerable.

✦ Lift dahlia tubers from pots, clean with a pastry brush and bury them in potting compost in a frost-free place.

MADE WITH LOVE

There's nothing more thoughtful than beautifully
wrapped gifts and handcrafted decorations

SET THE SCENE WITH GINGERBREAD

When you catch the gorgeous aroma of gingerbread baking, you know that the Christmas season has well and truly begun.
This classic Swedish variety Pepparkakor lasts well and has a great characteristic snap. You can, of course, use the dough
to make simple gingerbread people, rather than a garland, or just add one hole to each biscuit and hang individually

NATURAL NOËL

For an elegant look, wrap presents in gold or silver craft paper and tie with ribbon. To embellish, spray foraged acorns, pine cones and cuttings from the tree with white or silver spray paint, then tuck into the ribbon. Seal the gifts with double-sided or paper tape instead of sticky tape. ❂➤

GARLANDS GOOD ENOUGH TO EAT

DRIED CHILLI AND BAY TINSEL
Slow-dried chillies, dried in a very low oven overnight, retain a glorious red colour and last for months; use them to add a slightly smokey spice to dishes. Bay leaves are optional but create a festive look. String together using sewing thread and a sharp needle.

SNOWY PRETZELS
Dip large salted pretzels in melted chocolate and scatter over festive sprinkles. Leave to set completely before stringing with twine.

SPICED APPLE THINS
Finely slice 2 apples and pierce 2 holes in each slice. Toss with lemon juice, sprinkle with cinnamon and dry in a low oven for a few hours until leathery. Weave string through to hang.

Go with a bang!

Crackers are easier to make than you'd think.
Cut a 20 x 30cm piece of news or Christmas wrapping
paper, then stick double-sided tape on each long
side. Attach a toilet roll tube (with a prize, motto and
cracker snap tucked inside) to tape, roll up and secure
with the other piece of tape. Twist the ends and tie
with string, ensuring the snap stays centered.

Cracker jack

Add a touch of festive sparkle to a plain white cracker with a twist of
gold twine and a sprig of paper leaves decorated with circles of gold
glitter glue, which you can also use to adorn the ends of the cracker.

Decorate with scent

Fill your home with festive aromas by switching baubles for slices
of dried orange, sticks of cinnamon strung on ribbon and small
wreaths made from cardamon pods, hung on a mini tree.

Deck the halls

A garland of leaves makes a simple but stunning
decoration. Trace templates of various leaf shapes
(use the real thing) on to plain white and patterned
brown card, punch a hole in the top of each with a
hole-punch and string on to raffia straw ribbon. ➥

RING IN THE SEASON

Create a wreath that smells as good as it looks from a mix of eucalyptus, pine, sage, rosemary and thyme springs. To make, weave your stems through a wire wreath frame. Keep it natural or add pops of colour with holly and berries for a more traditional look.

3 PLANTS FOR WINTER DISPLAYS

Leaves and sprigs last much longer than fresh flowers

Rosemary

This beautifully scented herb is a great filler for winter bouquets. Keep it watered and it will last for several weeks.

Eucalyptus

This Australian plant adds fullness and a fresh scent to flower arrangements and lasts for up to three weeks in water. It also dries beautifully.

Mistletoe

This Christmas favourite works in wreaths, centrepieces, garlands or hung over a doorway. Look for stems with plump white berries and keep cool to preserve its freshness.

CHRISTMAS TIPPLE

To make this spiced liqueur, heat 75g **light muscovado sugar** and 200ml **water** in a small pan over low heat, stirring to dissolve. Add 3 **whole cloves**, 3 **bruised cardamom pods**, 2 **cinnamon sticks** (broken), ½ **star anise** and large pinch **freshly grated nutmeg**; bring to the boil. Cover and simmer for 10min. Remove from heat, add 350ml **vodka**, re-cover and leave overnight to infuse. Empty a 397g tin **Carnation Caramel** into a large jug and gradually whisk in 300ml **single cream**. Strain in the spiced vodka through a fine sieve (discard spices), add large pinch of salt and whisk to combine. Decant into sterilised bottles and chill. Makes 1ltr. ➥

THE BIG COUNTDOWN

For a home-made Advent calendar, create a hanging Christmas tree from lengths of foraged wood strung together in a triangle shape with velvet ribbon. Decorate with baubles and stars then tie on numbered presents (which can be themed or personalised), ready to open from 1 December.

It's a wrap

Handmade wrapping paper stands out for all the right reasons. Use a festive stamp (a fir tree or holly and berries dipped in red or green work well) in a repeated pattern on plain white or brown craft paper.

Merry & bright

These striking cards are easy to make: first cut out a bauble template and use to cut shapes in decorative paper. Tie colourful string into a bow through the top of the bauble. Fold thick white paper into cards, put the bauble in the centre of the front of the card, and loop the string ends over the top, securing with tape inside.

Painted pines

These watercolour cards are easier to paint than you think. Sketch a Christmas tree on watercolour paper in pencil, then dampen the paper. Mix your green, then paint in thin strokes from the outer edges of the tree, letting the colour bleed inwards. Add more water to spread the colour. Create definition with a darker green.

Special labels

Show you care with home-made gift tags, decorated with stamps, decoupage, ribbon and foraged leaves, bark and berries — extra points for personalising the design to match the recipient. ∎

BEAUTYWISE

It's the most wonderful time of the year, and a chance to celebrate in style, but party season doesn't have to mean spending hours in front of a mirror.

There are some 'going out, out' looks that are truly evergreen and easy to streamline, so you can then just relax and let your hair down...

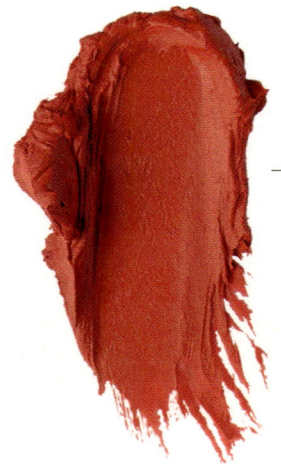

WINTER MUST-HAVE

Using a primer between your moisturiser and foundation will give your makeup far better staying power — and that's not all. Choose a product with a finish that matches your skin wishlist, whether that's radiance boosting or shine mattifying, and you'll elevate your overall look all night long as well.

DIY manicure tips

If you're applying nail polish yourself, remember that pale, matte shades are prone to streaking and often need multiple coats. Dark polishes with a metallic finish are easier to apply, forgiving on ridges and offer great coverage in one coat. For longest-lasting results, use a base and topcoat, but if your mani just needs to last a night, speed-set polish with quick-dry spray, a warm hairdryer or cold water.

Master a red lip

The secret to a great red lip? It's not lipstick! Your secret weapon is a red lip liner and the reason is three-fold. First, you can use it to create a neat shape that can be corrected before you go any further. Second, it creates a block against bleeding. Thirdly, you can then use the same lip liner to fill in your entire lip shape. As well as adding 'grip' to any lipstick you apply over the top, it also provides a comfortable yet durable base layer that will stay put even if your actual lippy fades. No more lipstick 'holes' after a few drinks.

DID YOU KNOW?

FOR LESS 'FALSE'-LOOKING FALSE LASHES, GO FOR 'UNDERLASHES', A FAVOURITE DIY TRICK OF CELEBRITY MAKEUP ARTISTS. THEY ATTACH IN CLUSTERS TO THE UNDERSIDE OF YOUR OWN LASHES, GIVING A COMPLETELY INVISIBLE JOIN AND AN UNDERSTATED, EYE-LIFTING LOOK.

A simple smokey eye

You can smoke it up with a 20-shade palette, or you can take this cheat's shortcut. Prep your lids with a medium-brown eyeshadow in your choice of shimmer or matte finish, then grab a soft, dark-brown eye pencil. Draw a sideways V shape, starting from your upper lash line then doubling back all along your creaseline. It doesn't need to be neat because you'll then use a small fluffy brush to blend all the edges away, so the pencil blurs into the eyeshadow. Outline your lower lashline with pencil, and blur again with the brush. Finish with a jet-black mascara, and you're done.

PERFECT BROWS

For flattering, face-framing brows in a flash, focus on fullness, not darkness. A brow powder is the most foolproof way to add structure in a natural-looking way. Tap off any excess product, then apply it with a small brush in light, feathery strokes, starting at the arch before extending to the tail and then finishing at the front of the brow. This cleverly avoids the common mistake of being too heavy-handed at the inner edges. Finish with a clear brow gel, brushing brows upwards and outwards for a youthful effect.

FASHIONWISE

Bring out the big guns! Winter is the season when function truly meets fashion. It's when your coat becomes part of your identity, and your hat, gloves and boots become style statements. This is when you'll be glad of all the heavy hitters you've invested in over the years – and one of winter's joys is assembling them back into play once again.

WARDROBE KNOW-HOW

Give coats a refresh with a fabric brush or a dry clean if needed, and check zips, fastenings and linings. Wash hats, scarves and gloves (you'd be surprised how grubby they get), and match up any solo gloves. Padded gilets and shearling-lined waistcoats are the real heroes when it comes to mastering indoor/outdoor comfort. They work thrown over jumpers when the house is chilly, as well as under looser-fit coats, adding warmth without bulk. Thermal base layers deserve a shout-out too: invisible, essential and worth their weight in gold.

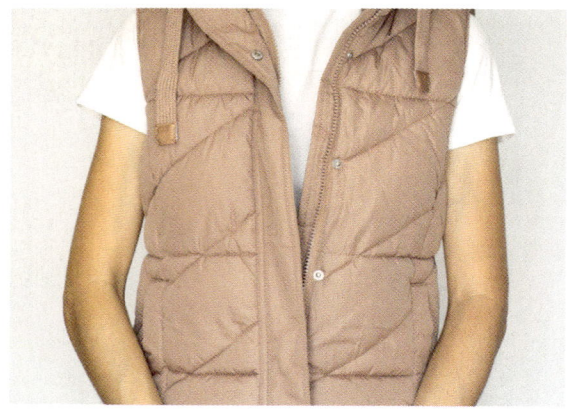

BUY NOW, WEAR NOW

Invest in a great pair of sturdy jeans. The right pair will work with puffers, knits, shearling boots and everything in between. Look for a mid-to-high rise, and a straight or slightly tapered leg, as well as a bit of stretch for comfort. Darker washes feel wintry, but black or inky indigo pairs are the most versatile.

Shapewise

Yes, your puffer can be stylish. Go for a slightly cropped version to wear with jeans and chunky boots, or a belted style to define your waist. Monochrome keeps things sleek, or try colour blocking for a sporty edge. Keep the silhouette streamlined underneath – slim trousers or leggings work better than lots of volume.

What makes a good...
WINTER COAT?

This is the one piece you'll wear more than any other – so make it count. The best winter coats have:

✦ A water-resistant or waterproof outer layer
✦ Insulation (down or a good quality synthetic fill)
✦ A hood – ideally one that is detachable or adjustable
✦ Secure pockets (bonus if they're fleece-lined for cold hands)
✦ A length that covers your thighs for the coldest days and nights

If you're active, look for storm cuffs, two-way zips and ventilation options. Choose a neutral tone if it's your only coat – or a bold colour if you want to brighten up grey days.

DID YOU KNOW?

THE PUFFER JACKET (OR DOWN COAT) WAS INVENTED IN THE 1930s BY EDDIE BAUER, AFTER HE NEARLY DIED OF HYPOTHERMIA ON A FISHING TRIP. HE FILLED THE JACKET WITH GOOSE DOWN - INSPIRED BY BEDDING - AND THE REST IS (COSY) HISTORY. ∎

HEALTHWISE

The clocks have gone back and the temperature has dropped. Winter is here – and with it comes unwelcome seasonal visitors like coughs, colds and dips in energy. That's why taking a few simple steps to protect your health will really pay off, helping you feel energised, focussed and lurgy-free.

3 VITAMIN-RICH WINTER SALADS

Warming white salad

A great-for-your-gut combination with antioxidant-rich chicory, and Stilton, which contains beneficial live bacteria that can act as a gut-friendly probiotic.
HOW TO MAKE IT: Chop two heads of **chicory** and 1 **pear**. Crumble 50g **Stilton** over the top. Drizzle over a dressing of **wholegrain mustard**, **cider vinegar**, **honey** and **extra virgin olive oil**.

Mackerel and kale salad

Oily fish is packed with omega-3 fatty acids, protein and essential vitamins and minerals; cruciferous kale is rich in vitamins C and E, plus selenium and beta-carotene to boost immunity.
HOW TO MAKE IT: Scatter 150g chopped **kale** leaves (discarding the stalks) on a baking sheet lined with baking paper. Drizzle with 2tbsp **olive oil**, sprinkle with **salt** and bake at 180°C for 10mins. Make a dressing by mixing the juice of 1 **lemon**, 150ml **soured cream** and 2tbsp **creamed horseradish**. Score skin of 2 **mackerel fillets**, rub with oil and place skin-side up under a hot grill for 5mins or until cooked. Combine 500g cooked **puy lentils**, 250g chopped cooked **beetroot** and the kale chips. Top with the mackerel and drizzle with dressing.

Festive slaw

Red cabbage is rich in anthocyanins, antioxidants that can help lower blood pressure, reduce LDL (bad) cholesterol and improve blood vessel flexibility, while pumpkin seeds contain zinc, a mineral crucial for immune function.
HOW TO MAKE IT: Finely slice ½ **red cabbage**, ½ **apple**, ½ **red onion** and 2 grated **carrots**. Mix with **flat-leaf parsley** and a dressing of **olive oil** and **lemon juice**. Scatter **dried cranberries** and **pumpkin seeds** over the top.

Health hack

Reach for the walnuts at breakfast time. Researchers at the University of Reading found that eating 50g walnuts at the start of the day led to faster reaction times and better memory performance later on, when compared to eating breakfast without nuts. Why? It's all down to the walnut's unique mix of nutrients – a combination of omega-3 fatty acids, polyphenols and protein, which all support brain function, particularly memory.

FITNESS FOCUS

It can be tough to motivate yourself to get to the gym in winter, which is why it's the perfect season for effective workouts you can do at home. There are free tutorials on YouTube and apps for every type of exercise but, for expert advice, interactive fitness plans and access to more than 2,000 workouts, try joining the *Women's Health* Collective, the free, five-week NHS Strength and Flex exercise plan or the NHS Couch to 5K running programme.

IF YOU ONLY DO ONE THING...

Take a sauna. Evidence suggests regular saunas may offer some protection from dementia, help lung function and provide a significant boost to mood. They're also surprisingly effective at reducing blood pressure – one study showed a 30-minute sauna led to significantly lower readings.

DID YOU KNOW?

HAVING PORRIDGE FOR BREAKFAST IS LINKED TO SUSTAINED ENERGY LEVELS AND ALERTNESS THANKS TO IT BEING HIGH IN COMPLEX CARBOHYDRATES WITH LIMITED SUGAR. ∎

NOTEBOOK

TO DO

At home

1

2

3

4

5

In the kitchen

1

2

3

4

5

In the garden

1

2

3

4

5

For myself

1

2

3

4

5

THIS WINTER I'VE BEEN GRATEFUL FOR...

'WINTER IS A SEASON OF RECOVERY AND PREPARATION'
Paul Theroux

DIARY

NOTEBOOK

TO DO

At home

1
2
3
4
5

In the kitchen

1
2
3
4
5

In the garden

1
2
3
4
5

For myself

1
2
3
4
5

THIS AUTUMN I'VE BEEN GRATEFUL FOR...

'EVERY LEAF SPEAKS BLISS TO ME,
FLUTTERING FROM THE AUTUMN TREE'
Emily Brontë

September _____

1ST ____	2ND ____	3RD ____	4TH ____	5TH ____	6TH ____	7TH ____	8TH ____
9TH ____	10TH ____	11TH ____	12TH ____	13TH ____	14TH ____	15TH ____	16TH ____
17TH ____	18TH ____	19TH ____	20TH ____	21ST ____	22ND ____	23RD ____	24TH ____
25TH ____	26TH ____	27TH ____	28TH ____	29TH ____	30TH ____		

October _____

1ST ____	2ND ____	3RD ____	4TH ____	5TH ____	6TH ____	7TH ____	8TH ____
9TH ____	10TH ____	11TH ____	12TH ____	13TH ____	14TH ____	15TH ____	16TH ____
17TH ____	18TH ____	19TH ____	20TH ____	21ST ____	22ND ____	23RD ____	24TH ____
25TH ____	26TH ____	27TH ____	28TH ____	29TH ____	30TH ____	31ST ____	

November _____

1ST ____	2ND ____	3RD ____	4TH ____	5TH ____	6TH ____	7TH ____	8TH ____
9TH ____	10TH ____	11TH ____	12TH ____	13TH ____	14TH ____	15TH ____	16TH ____
17TH ____	18TH ____	19TH ____	20TH ____	21ST ____	22ND ____	23RD ____	24TH ____
25TH ____	26TH ____	27TH ____	28TH ____	29TH ____	30TH ____		

WINTER

As the nights draw in and the days get chillier, nature sleeps. The festive season brings us cheer and we look forward with hope to the year ahead of us

The coldest season with the shortest days. When stepping outside means wrapping up warm against bitter temperatures and brisk winds. But winter can also be enchanting, as nature throws a blanket of pristine snow over the land and paints our gardens in frosted filigree. As American naturalist John Burroughs said: 'He who marvels at the beauty of the world in summer will find equal cause for wonder and admiration in winter.'

Green globes of mistletoe are easier to spot now that most trees have shed their leaves. Snowdrops peek from the soil like bright white gems. And once the weather turns crisp and clear, sounds seem sharper, stars brighter and robins braver as they hop into our gardens in search of food. Look to the skies at sunset to see a murmuration of starlings, swooping, swirling and shape-shifting in a mesmerising winter aerial display. ↱

December, January, February. The winter months may seem long but they're filled with festivities, starting with Christmas, a time for friends and families to eat, drink and be merry (usually in that order!).

Shops, homes and high streets sparkle with fairy lights. Carols are sung, we watch *Love, Actually* or *Elf* (again!) and Mariah Carey makes a small fortune. It's not always perfect, and we rarely get a gift we actually want, but we love it anyway and find ways to celebrate the joy and discover meaning in the chaos.

Christmas trees are hung with our favourite family decorations (who cares how tacky the tinsel is?), halls are decked, wreaths are made and the turkey is ordered. Festive feasting is what we look forward to most and hosting is how we care for the ones we love. Planners make puddings, mince pies and cakes on stir-up Sunday, filling the kitchen with aromas of sweet, fruity spiciness. The rest of us panic and buy them in the 'big Christmas shop' but who's judging?

Children write letters to Santa (although he's on social media now, too) and hang stockings

> 'ALL YOU NEED IS A COSY COAT AND BOBBLE HAT TO ENJOY WALKS AND SLEDGING'

on Christmas Eve, waiting with one eye open for his arrival.

If we're lucky enough to get a smattering of snow (the odds of a white Christmas are roughly 50/50) we'll rush out to earn those rosy cheeks. All you need is a cosy coat, bobble hat and gloves to enjoy walks, sledging and snowball fights in a sparkling winter wonderland.

Next up? New Year. And whether you're a party animal or prefer watching the fireworks on TV, thoughts turn to what the next year might bring. While it's great to make resolutions, keep your goals achievable so you won't be so easily defeated – small and positive steps are more likely to power you on. And rather than make it all about joining a gym or giving up carbs, throw in some imagination and promise yourself you'll visit somewhere you've always wanted to go or learn something you've never tried before.

Come February, romance blooms for Valentine's Day. Declarations are made, roses are delivered and love tokens shared. But what also warms our hearts is knowing that spring is just around the corner, ready to burst into life once again. ∎

PLANNER

Dates to remember

Make a note of any birthdays, holidays, celebrations or appointments you have in the months of December, January and February.

Winter goals

1

2

3

4

5

Notes

Did you know?

First-footing is a common Scottish and Manx tradition on New Year's Eve. The first-footer is the first person to cross the threshold of someone's home after midnight on New Year's Day, and gifts such as shortbread, whisky or coal (to symbolise a warm home) are often given to bring good luck for the year ahead. Traditionally, the luckiest first-footer was a dark-haired man, while fair-headed men were considered the unluckiest – possibly stemming from past fears of Viking invasion!

WINTER IN NUMBERS

9

The fastest speed in miles per hour that a snowflake can fall.

5:1

The ratio of snow to water that scientists have calculated is ideal for building a snowman.

1,000

The number of ladybirds that typically gather in a 'huddle', the form of hibernation insects use.

-27.2°C

The coldest temperature recorded in the UK – in 1895, then in 1982 and again in 1995.

421

The number of words Scots have for snow – including *sneesl*, *skelf* and *snaw-pouther*.

BRUSSELS SPROUTS

Love them or hate them, these bulbous brassicas
are a winter staple and surprisingly good for our gut

A CHRISTMAS TRADITION

Synonymous with festive dining, Brussels sprouts deserve to be embraced beyond lunch on 25 December. Named after the capital of Belgium, where they were a popular crop from the 16th century, they belong to the same cruciferous family as cabbages. With a polarising reputation due to their characteristic mild bitterness, chewing them creates sulforaphane, which not only gives sprouts their unique flavour but also helps neutralise toxins and calm inflammation in the body. Plus, Brussels pack more vitamin C than oranges and offer a great source of vitamin K, folic acid, manganese and dietary fibre. When buying, look for plump green spheres – the smaller, the sweeter. If still on the stalk, twist off sprouts individually and peel off any yellow outer leaves. Trim the bases and leave the smaller sprouts whole. Some people like to cut a cross in the bases of larger ones; some simply halve them. Steam, boil or roast just until tender – be aware that a sulphur-like smell is a sure sign they've been overcooked! ❧

GH TIP

This also works well with crispy bacon lardons in place of the smoked salmon. Fry until crispy before adding in step 3.

CREAMY SPROUT, SALMON AND GNOCCHI GRATIN

A rich and hearty comfort food dish that even sprout haters will love. Use Cheddar if you don't have (or like) Gruyère.

Hands-on time: 25min. Cooking time: about 45min. Serves 4

40g butter, plus extra
to grease
40g plain flour
2tsp thyme leaves
400ml milk
100g Gruyère, grated
200g Brussels sprouts, halved
500g fresh gnocchi
50g smoked salmon trimmings
25g Parmesan, finely grated

1. Preheat oven to 220°C (200°C) mark 7. Melt butter in a medium pan, add flour and thyme and cook on low heat, stirring, for 2min. Gradually stir in milk, to make a smooth sauce. Bring slowly to the boil, stirring, until thickened. Remove from heat and stir in Gruyère and seasoning. Set aside.
2. Grease a 2 litre serving dish.

Bring a large pan of salted water to the boil, add sprouts and simmer for 5min until just tender. Using a slotted spoon, scoop out to a sieve to drain. Add gnocchi to the pan, return to the boil and simmer for 2min until bobbing and tender. Drain.
3. Halve cooked sprouts and mix with gnocchi and salmon in the serving dish. Pour over cheese sauce and sprinkle with Parmesan. Cook in oven for 25min or until browned. Serve with a crisp green salad.
PER SERVING *494cals, 21g protein, 23g fat (13g saturates), 50g carbs (7g total sugars), 3g fibre.* ∎

FOODWISE

Far from matching the grey and bleak weather outside, the winter kitchen is an explosion of colour, with vibrant pink rhubarb, bright orange clementines and rich green savoys all jostling to be cooked with. From zingy winter salads, to comforting puddings, this season is all about bringing joy to our tables – and that's before we even think about Christmas dinner!

IN SEASON

SAVOY CABBAGE
Named after the Savoy region in France, savoy cabbage is known for its dark green crinkly leaves and is best between October and February. Look for tightly packed heads, firm to the touch. Its slightly sweeter taste needs little cooking – sauté shredded leaves in butter or roast wedges in the oven.

JERUSALEM ARTICHOKES
Part of the sunflower family and native to North America, these knobbly tubers are like a sweeter, nuttier potato – great roasted, mashed, puréed or in velvety soup. Best soon after harvest but hardy enough to stay in the ground until needed.

CLEMENTINES
Typically grown in warmer European climes, clementines peak between November and January. A festive favourite, the citrus balances well with the seasonal richness. Choose bright orange fruits that feel heavy.

FORCED RHUBARB
Famed for its vibrant pink hue, forced rhubarb comes into its prime in late winter, typically available from late December to early March. Grown in dark, damp forcing sheds only by candlelight, it grows quickly in search of light, producing the characteristic long pink stems, which are sweeter than summer rhubarb.

BLOOD ORANGES
Normally grown in Europe with a short season, so grab them in January and February. Smaller and sweeter than regular oranges, they're known for their ruby red flesh that develops after a drop in night-time temperatures.

DID YOU KNOW?

FORCED RHUBARB IS MAINLY GROWN IN THE RHUBARB TRIANGLE IN WEST YORKSHIRE, WHICH HAS PDO (PROTECTED DESIGNATION OF ORIGIN) STATUS.

Batch cooking hacks

Whether you're getting ahead for Christmas or prepping for chilly nights when you want to heat up something warming, winter is the time to embrace getting ahead...

✦ Before you set out on a batch-cooking marathon, be sure you've decluttered your freezer of anything that has passed its best.

✦ Check you have plenty of suitable freezer containers to hand that are both the right material (some plastics don't like the cold!) and the right size – otherwise you'll waste space. Freezer bags are great for soups and sauces as they take up less room.

✦ If you're put off batch cooking by the repetitiveness of having the same dish time and time again, choose a base that's very easy to twist up. A good beef ragu is great with pasta, but can be pimped with a big dollop of chipotle paste and a can of kidney beans for a delicious chilli, too.

3 WAYS TO BRIGHTEN UP DISHES

Quick and easy ideas to make the most of the winter harvest

1
For a really easy pudding, roast forced rhubarb with a touch of sugar until tender, then toss with finely chopped stem ginger and some ginger syrup. Serve with Greek yogurt and a ginger snap on the side.

2
For a tasty winter salad, griddle blood orange segments until just caramelised, then toss through a salad of dressed radicchio and walnuts, crumbling in some goat's cheese to serve.

3
For the easiest pasta dish, sauté bacon lardons in butter, tossing in some shredded savoy cabbage when the bacon starts to crisp. Once the cabbage is tender, toss through freshly cooked pasta with a dollop of crème fraîche. Season well. ∎

SEASON'S FEASTINGS

It's the most anticipated meal of the year, so make yours magical with our Triple-Tested recipes for turkey and all the trimmings

MENU

FOR 8

*Ham Hock Terrine with
Cider Jelly*

*Maple and Clementine
Turkey with Sherry Gravy*

*Honey Mustard
Chantenay Carrots,
Buttered Brussels,
Garlic and Sage Roast
Potatoes, Dressed Green
Beans, Roast Cabbage
with Blue Cheese
Dressing, Crispy Topped
Sprouts, Stacked
Potato Dauphinoise,
Rice Stuffing Cakes*

*Hasselback Squash
(vegetarian)*

*Gingerbread Christmas
Pudding with Ginger
Caramel Sauce*

MAPLE AND CLEMENTINE TURKEY WITH SHERRY GRAVY

Hands-on time: 45min, plus coming up to room temperature and resting. Cooking time: about 3¼hr. Serves 8, with leftovers

5.4kg free-range turkey
4 clementines, plus extra to garnish (optional)
125g butter, softened
8 thyme sprigs, plus extra (optional) to garnish
2 fat garlic cloves, crushed
3tbsp maple syrup
2 large onions, skin on, thickly sliced
FOR THE GRAVY
25g plain flour
150ml dry sherry

1. One hour before cooking, remove turkey from fridge and remove any wrappings, giblets or trussing. Pat dry with kitchen paper and use tweezers to pluck out any stray feathers. Allow turkey to come up to room temperature. Weigh the turkey and calculate the cooking time, allowing 30-35min per kg.

2. Preheat oven to 190°C (170°C fan) mark 5. Finely grate zest of 2 of the clementines into a medium bowl. Halve the zested and unzested clementines and set aside. To the zest bowl, add the softened butter, the leaves from half the thyme sprigs, the garlic, maple syrup and some seasoning. Mix.

3. Lift up turkey neck flap and use your fingers to ease the skin gently away from some of the breast meat. Work half the butter mixture under the skin, and over the breast. Place the zested, halved clementines and remaining thyme sprigs in the central turkey cavity.

4. Make a trivet in a large, sturdy roasting tin with onion slices. Loosely tie turkey legs together with kitchen string and rub remaining flavoured butter all over the bird. Add remaining halved clementines to the tin along with 100ml water and loosely cover tin with foil.

5. Roast for calculated time, basting occasionally. Remove foil for last 30min of cooking. To check the turkey is cooked, insert a fork into the thickest part of the breast and check that the juices run golden and clear. If there's any red tinge to the juice, return to the oven and keep checking every 10min. Or use a meat thermometer – the temperature needs to read at least 72°C when inserted into the thickest part of the breast.

6. Transfer turkey to a board (set aside the roasting tin for gravy); cover well with foil and then clean tea towels to help keep the heat in. Leave to rest in a warm place for at least 30min or up to 1¼hr.

7. Make the gravy. Spoon off all but about 2tbsp excess fat from the roasting tin (leaving other roasting remains in tin). Put tin over medium hob heat and whisk in flour, mashing the onion and clementines as you go. Cook, whisking, for 1min. Whisk in the sherry (scraping up all the sticky bits from the base of the tin) and leave to bubble for a few min. Whisk in 350ml water and leave to simmer, whisking occasionally, for a couple of min until thickened. Strain into a warmed gravy jug or clean pan (to reheat when needed). Check seasoning.

8. To serve, unwrap turkey and transfer to a warm platter. Garnish with extra thyme sprigs and fried clementine wedges, if you like. Serve with gravy.

PER 125G MEAT & 50ML GRAVY
264cals, 39g protein, 11g fat (4g saturates), 1g carbs (0g total sugars), 0g fibre ●➤

GET AHEAD

Prepare steps 2-4 up to a day ahead (don't preheat oven). Place turkey into a sturdy roasting tin or on a tray. Cover and chill. To serve, complete step 1 and continue with step 4.

HAM HOCK TERRINE WITH CIDER JELLY

Hands-on time: 45min, plus cooling and overnight chilling. Cooking time: about 3hr 20min. Serves 8

2.6kg gammon hocks
(also called knuckles),
check with your butcher
that they're cured, and buy
the best quality meat you can
500ml apple juice
4 bay leaves
1 onion, roughly chopped
Small handful thyme sprigs
1tsp black peppercorns
Oil, to grease
Large handful parsley, finely
chopped
2tbsp wholegrain mustard
1tbsp capers, rinsed
3 gelatine leaves
200ml cider, to serve
Fruity chutney or onion
marmalade
Caper berries, optional
Toasts

1. Put the gammon hocks into a large pan and add the apple juice, bay leaves, onion, thyme and peppercorns. Add cold water to cover. Bring to the boil, then turn down the heat and simmer for 2½-3hr, topping up the water as needed, until the hocks are tender and the meat is falling from the bone. Leave hocks to cool in the liquid for about 1hr, then lift out (reserve liquid).
2. Strain liquid into a clean pan through a fine sieve and boil fiercely to reduce to about 500ml. Set aside. Lightly oil a 900g loaf tin and line with a couple of layers of clingfilm, making sure there is plenty hanging over the sides (to make removal easier).
3. Remove and discard the skin from the hocks and finely shred the meat – you should have about 700g. Discard any fatty or sinewy bits.
4. Put hock into a bowl and mix in parsley, mustard and capers. Spoon into tin, pressing down. Chill.
5. Put gelatine into a pan and cover with the cider. Leave to soak for 5min. Heat gently to dissolve the gelatine. Take off heat, add the reduced cooking liquid and check seasoning.
6. Slowly pour the liquid into the tin, allowing it to seep in until it's just covering the meat (you might not need all of the liquid). Cover tin with clingfilm (make sure it doesn't touch the liquid) and chill overnight.
7. To serve, unwrap clingfilm and invert on to a serving platter or board. Lift off tin and peel off clingfilm. Spoon some chutney or onion marmalade on top and decorate with caper berries, if using. Serve with toasts.
PER SERVING *(without chutney and toasts) 164cals, 17g protein, 7g fat (2g saturates), 7g carbs (7g total sugars), 0g fibre*

GARLIC AND SAGE ROAST POTATOES

Hands-on time: 20min. Cooking time: about 1½hr. Serves 8

2kg floury potatoes
7tbsp olive oil or goose fat
6 garlic cloves (skin on)
Small handful sage leaves

1. Preheat oven to 190°C (170°C fan) mark 5. Peel potatoes and cut into large even-sized pieces. Put into a large pan and cover with cold salted water. Cover pan, bring to boil. Uncover and simmer for 8-10min.
2. Meanwhile, heat oil/fat in a large roasting tin in the oven. Drain potatoes into a colander and leave for 2min. Rough up potato edges.
3. Carefully pour potatoes into the hot oil/fat, turning to coat. Add garlic cloves and some seasoning. Roast for 1-1¼hr until golden and cooked through, basting/turning occasionally, and adding the sage for the final 30min of cooking. Serve in a warm serving dish.
PER SERVING *305cals, 5g protein, 10g fat (2g saturates), 47g carbs (2g total sugars), 5g fibre* ➡

Add carrots (no need to peel!) and mix to coat. Add a splash of water to the tin, cover with foil and roast for 30min, shaking halfway through.
2. Uncover and cook for a further 20-30min until caramelised and tender. Stir the carrots to coat thoroughly in the glaze, transfer to warm serving dish and serve.
PER SERVING *92cals, 1g protein, 3g fat (0g saturates), 12g carbs (11g total sugars), 5g fibre*

CRISPY TOPPED SPROUTS

Hands-on time: 20min. Cooking time: about 15min. Serves 8

900g Brussels sprouts, trimmed and outer leaves removed, if needed
2tbsp olive oil
100g bacon lardons
FOR THE PANGRATTATO
25g butter
40g fresh white breadcrumbs
Finely grated zest 1 lemon

1. Bring a large pan of water to the boil and cook sprouts for 3min until nearly tender. Drain and plunge into cold water. Drain well and dry on kitchen paper. Halve any large sprouts.
2. Meanwhile, heat butter in a large, deep frying pan. Add breadcrumbs, stir to coat. Toast gently until golden and crisp, stirring constantly. Season lightly and stir in lemon zest, then empty on to a plate.

3. Wipe out the pan and return to the heat. Add oil and lardons, fry for a few minutes until beginning to caramelise. Add sprouts, increase heat to high and fry 5-7min, tossing until crisp and browned. Transfer to warm serving dish and scatter with pangrattato. Serve.
PER SERVING *54cals, 6g protein, 10g fat (3g saturates), 7g carbs (4g total sugars), 6g fibre*

HONEY MUSTARD CHANTENAY CARROTS

Hands-on time: 10min. Cooking time: about 1hr. Serves 8

2tbsp rapeseed or olive oil
2tbsp runny honey
1tbsp wholegrain mustard
1kg Chantenay carrots, washed and trimmed
1. Preheat oven to 190°C (170°C fan) mark 5. Mix oil, honey, mustard and seasoning in base of a roasting tin.

DRESSED GREEN BEANS

Hands-on time: 15min. Cooking time: about 10min. Serves 8

750g fine green beans, trimmed
50g walnuts, chopped
40g Comté cheese, shaved
FOR THE DRESSING
1½tbsp Dijon mustard
1½tbsp white wine vinegar
3tbsp olive oil
1 shallot, finely sliced

1. Bring a large pan of water to the boil. Simmer beans for 5min until just tender.
2. Meanwhile, whisk together the dressing ingredients with some seasoning in a small bowl.
3. Drain the beans well. Empty into a serving bowl and toss through the dressing, walnuts and Comté. Serve.
PER SERVING *135cals, 5g protein, 11g fat (2g saturates), 3g carbs (2g total sugars), 4g fibre*

'LET YOUR CHRISTMAS SIDE DISHES STEAL THE SHOW WITH BOLD, FESTIVE FLAVOURS AND PLENTY LEFT OVER FOR SECOND HELPINGS'

STACKED POTATO DAUPHINOISE

Hands-on time: 30min. Cooking time: about 1hr. Serves 8

6 large baking potatoes, peeled
300ml double cream
100ml chicken or vegetable stock
2 garlic cloves, crushed
½tsp freshly grated nutmeg
25g butter, plus extra
to grease

1. Preheat oven to 190°C (170°C fan) mark 5. Grease an ovenproof serving dish that fits all the whole peeled potatoes snugly. Finely slice the potatoes on a mandolin and place in a large bowl. Add cream, stock, garlic, nutmeg and seasoning and mix with hands. Arrange the slices into the dish, packing in rows.
2. Pour over remaining cream mixture; dot over butter. Cover tightly with foil; cook for 30min. Remove foil; cook for 30-35min more until potatoes are tender (test by piercing with a knife) and top is deep brown and crisp. Serve.
PER SERVING *375cals, 5g protein,*
23g fat (14g saturates), 36g carbs
(2g total sugars), 4g fibre

BUTTERED BRUSSELS

Hands-on time: 10min. Cooking time: about 15min. Serves 8

900g Brussels sprouts,
trimmed and outer leaves
removed, if needed
FOR THE BUTTER
25g butter, softened
25g flaked almonds, toasted
2tbsp chopped chives

1. Bring a large pan of water to the boil and cook sprouts for 5min until tender.
2. Meanwhile, mix butter ingredients with seasoning.
3. Drain sprouts, return to the pan and toss through the butter. Check seasoning, transfer to a warm serving dish and serve.
PER SERVING *104cals, 5g protein,*
6g fat (2g saturates), 5g carbs
(4g total sugars), 6g fibre

ROAST CABBAGE WITH BLUE CHEESE DRESSING

Hands-on time: 10min. Cooking time: about 35min. Serves 8

1 red cabbage, outer leaves
discarded
2tbsp vegetable oil
100g blue cheese, crumbled,
we used Stilton
75g soured cream
2tsp cider or white wine vinegar
½tsp Dijon mustard
4tbsp pomegranate seeds

1. Preheat oven to 220°C (200°C fan) mark 7 and line a baking tray with baking parchment. Cut cabbage in half through the core, then cut each half into 4 even wedges and put on the lined tray.
2. Drizzle with the oil, season and rub over the wedges to coat. Lay flat and cook for 30-35min, turning over halfway, until browned and tender.
3. Meanwhile, mash blue cheese with the soured cream to make a chunky sauce. Stir in vinegar, mustard and some seasoning.
4. Transfer cabbage wedges to a warmed serving plate and serve hot with the blue cheese sauce and pomegranate seeds spooned over.
PER SERVING *119cals, 4g protein,*
9g fat (4g saturates), 4g carbs
(3g total sugars), 2g fibre ➤

GET AHEAD

Vegetables such as
Brussels sprouts, potatoes
and carrots can be
prepped in advance
and kept fresh in
a bowl of cold water until
you're ready to cook them.

RICE STUFFING CAKES WITH HAZELNUT AND CRANBERRY

Hands-on time: 20min. Cooking time: about 50min. Makes 8

100g butter, plus extra to grease
3 banana shallots, finely chopped
250g pouch microwave basmati rice
50g chopped roasted hazelnuts, plus extra to garnish
100g dried cranberries, chopped
Handful parsley, roughly chopped
2 medium eggs, beaten

1. Preheat oven to 190°C (170°C fan) mark 5. Grease 8 holes of a muffin tin with butter and line each with strips of baking parchment, making sure they stick well above the edges of the tin (this will make removing the cakes easy).
2. Melt butter in a frying pan over low heat and fry shallots with a pinch of salt for 5min, until softened. Take pan off heat, add rice, stirring gently to break up any clumps, then stir in the hazelnuts, cranberries, parsley, eggs and plenty of seasoning. Spoon into prepared tins, packing down tightly.
3. Cook for 35-40min until golden. Run a palette knife around the edge of each stuffing cake and use the parchment to help lift out while piping hot. Transfer to a warm serving plate, scatter with extra hazelnuts and serve.
PER SERVING *294cals, 9g protein, 18g fat (7g saturates), 22g carbs (10g total sugars), 5g fibre*

GET AHEAD

Prepare to end of step 2 up to 2hr ahead (don't preheat oven). Cover and chill. To serve, preheat oven, uncover and complete recipe.

HASSELBACK SQUASH

For vegans, replace goat's cheese with a non-dairy cheese alternative.

Hands-on time: 20min. Cooking time: about 1¾hr. Serves 2-3 as a main, or 8 as a side.

1 butternut squash
1tbsp olive oil
1tbsp maple syrup
2 large thyme sprigs
75g goat's cheese, crumbled
1tbsp chopped roasted hazelnuts

1. Preheat oven to 190°C (170°C fan) mark 5. Peel the squash. Halve lengthways and scoop out the seeds. Place cut-side down on a board. Working one half at a time, make slices across the width of the squash, about 5mm (¼in) apart. You want to slice deep into the squash, but not all the way through.
2. Line a small baking tray with baking parchment. Lay on the squash halves, with the cuts facing up. Mix oil and maple syrup with some seasoning. Drizzle over the squash halves, working into the cuts. Lay a thyme sprig on each.
3. Roast for 1¼-1½hr, until tender but not collapsing (you should be able to push a knife through the thickest part).
4. Sprinkle over the cheese and hazelnuts and return to oven for 15min. Transfer to a warm serving plate and serve.
PER SERVING *(if serving 3) 242cals, 8g protein, 14g fat (5g saturates), 20g carbs (12g total sugars), 5g fibre* ❯❯

'THE SECRET TO HASSELBACK SLICING IS TO PLACE THE SQUASH BETWEEN TWO WOODEN SPOON HANDLES - IT WILL STOP THE KNIFE CUTTING THROUGH THE SKIN'

GET AHEAD

Prepare to end of step 3 up to 3hr ahead. Cool. Complete recipe to serve.

TO FLAME YOUR PUDDING

Pour 50ml (2fl oz) brandy, rum or whisky into a large metal ladle. Warm carefully over a low (gas) hob (if you don't have a gas hob, heat in a small pan first, then transfer to the ladle). Carefully light the brandy using a long match and slowly pour over the pudding.

GINGERBREAD CHRISTMAS PUDDING

We've warmed up our Christmas pudding with gingerbread spices. A finishing drizzle of luscious ginger caramel adds wow factor.

Hands-on time: 25min, plus overnight soaking, cooling and maturing. Cooking time: about 4½hr. Serves 8

175g raisins
175g sultanas
100g Medjool dates, stoned and finely chopped
25g chopped mixed peel
100ml apple juice
50ml brandy
Butter, to grease
150g grated apple
2tsp ground cinnamon
2tsp mixed spice
2tsp ground ginger
3 balls stem ginger, drained and finely chopped
100 dark brown soft sugar
75g treacle
75g golden syrup
100g plain flour
75g fresh white breadcrumbs
1 large egg, beaten
25g vegetarian suet

1. Put the dried fruit, mixed peel, apple juice and brandy into a large non-metallic bowl. Mix, cover and leave to soak overnight at room temperature.
2. Grease a 900ml pudding basin and line the base with a disc of baking parchment. Put a 30.5cm square of foil on top of a square of baking parchment of the same size. Fold a 4cm pleat in the centre and set aside.
3. Add remaining ingredients to the soaked fruit, mixing well. Transfer to the basin and press down. Put the foil and parchment (foil side up) on top and smooth down to cover. Tie a long piece of string securely under the lip of the basin and loop over the top to create a handle.
4. To cook, put a heatproof saucer into a large pan that has a tight-fitting lid. Lower in the pudding and pour in water to halfway up the sides of the basin. Cover with the lid, bring to a boil and simmer for 4½hr, topping up the water as necessary.
5. Remove the pudding from the pan and leave to cool completely. Wrap the entire basin in a layer of clingfilm followed by a layer of foil. Store in a cool, dark place and leave to mature for up to 2 months.
PER SERVING *408cals, 5g protein, 4g fat (2g saturates), 83g carbs (68g total sugars), 3g fibre*

TO REHEAT

Remove clingfilm and foil and re-cover with a new lid as per instructions in steps 2 and 3. Following method in step 4, steam for 1½hr until piping hot in the centre when pierced with a skewer. Remove from the pan and leave to sit for 5min. Remove lid and invert on to a serving plate. Peel off baking parchment and serve with Ginger Caramel Sauce, if you like.

GINGER CARAMEL SAUCE

Heat 50g **caster sugar** with 50ml water in a heavy-bottomed pan, stirring, until sugar dissolves. Turn up the heat and bubble until a deep caramel colour – do not stir, rather swirl the pan. Remove from heat and slowly stir in 150ml **double cream**, followed by 15g **unsalted butter** and 3tbsp **ginger syrup** (from a jar of stem ginger). Return to the heat to dissolve any hardened sugar, stirring. Bubble for a couple of min. Take off heat. Cool slightly and serve warm or at room temperature over, or alongside, the pudding.
PER 1TBSP *74cals, 0g protein, 6g fat (4g saturates), 5g carbs (5g total sugars), 0g fibre* ■

'USE UP LEFTOVER CHRISTMAS PUD BY CRUMBLING IT INTO A TUB OF SOFTENED VANILLA ICE CREAM AND REFREEZING'

ALL SET FOR CHRISTMAS

Impress your guests and celebrate in style with
three of our favourite festive tablescapes

RICH ELEGANCE

Teaming deep red with gold adds glamour and sparkle to the traditional Christmas look – and you can never have too much of that! Dial up the richness with a sumptuous tablecloth and balance solid colour (on this table, the gold placemats and cutlery) with delicate accents (the gold-rimmed plates and glassware). Soft green foliage adds natural freshness to velvety red roses, glittery baubles and spray-painted leaves. For added grandeur, include tall candles in glass holders that catch the light, and make each place setting special with a simple decorative touch – a red sprig and glittery cone is all you need for a final festive flourish.➻

NATURAL CHARM

For a Christmas table that feels wonderfully relaxed yet still impressive, focus on earthy tones, tactile materials and understated tableware. There's no need for a tablecloth – a runner is the perfect base for a centrepiece created with a leafy garland, frosted pine cones and paper baubles. Add tea lights in rustic holders. Crumpled linen adds to the laid-back look and, in warm white, creates a welcoming table. Elevate the room with a dramatic floating centrepiece echoing the tablescape – hang a rod from the ceiling cascading greenery (such as faux eucalyptus, seen here) and paper or glass baubles in all sizes. Guaranteed to add some drama. ➻

BEYOND MIDNIGHT

Unusual colour combinations and textures will create a modern-looking Christmas table. Set shades of pale blue, olive green and rich teal against a vivid backdrop of midnight blue, with shots of metallic copper and bronze for added pizazz. Lime-green flowers in amber bud vases inject eye-catching pops of neon colour that provide a refreshing contrast to iridescent baubles and faux foliage in different shades of blue. Mix up your textures, too, with velvety ribbons and pleated paper baubles to soften and balance the look. For a final festive touch, add a curtain of warm white fairy lights, hanging them from the ceiling or across a wall, for a room full of joy. ∎

HOMEWISE

Winter is a season of two very different moods. It begins in December with plenty of festive cheer and ends with the dark, cold days of January and February. At home, after the New Year celebrations, we hunker down and yearn for the lightness of spring. How to keep your spirits up? By hanging on to some of that Christmas colour, warming up your walls and adding plenty of sparkling light.

GO LARGE

Oversized decorations deliver more festive bang for your buck. As well as honeycomb baubles, try giant 3D snowflakes and stars. Group one type together for most impact, hanging them at different lengths from the ceiling above a table, in a window, a corner or from a bannister or mantelpiece.

FAIRYLAND

Christmas isn't Christmas without fairy lights but choose ones with a warm white light instead of chilly blue. The latter have become more common since the introduction of LEDs but it's the old-fashioned style lights that deliver the lovely magical feel that's associated with Christmas. It also means you can enjoy your fairy lights well beyond 5 January, when their twinkly light will add much-needed cheer. Take them off your tree (perhaps even invest in a few more, including those that are battery-powered) and use them around the home instead; trailed along a mantelpiece, framing a mirror, piled into an unused fireplace, popped into large glass jars to light up a windowsill, threaded through a flower arrangement… essentially, anywhere a bit of sparkle will help to lighten up your day.

Home scents

Celebrate with fragrances capturing seasonal nostalgia such as clementine, cloves, frankincense and cinnamon. As winter deepens, lean into heavier and spicier fragrances including patchouli, pepper and leather.

Warmer walls

Decorate empty wall spaces by hanging up a throw or blanket (yes, really!) This insiders' decorating trick will instantly make a large blank space more interesting, as well as giving a room a warmer look and feel. Treat it like artwork – look for one in a pattern you love and that fits with your existing decor. Hang it using adhesive strips or fix it to a wooden dowel and mount on brackets.

WINTER BUY

Winter's lack of natural light lowers mood for many, even without SAD (Seasonal Affective Disorder). Use a SAD lamp emitting 2,500-10,000 lux (higher lux means brighter light). Half an hour daily sat in front of one prompts your brain to produce more serotonin, the feelgood hormone. ∎

TO-DO LIST

At this time of year, life starts to get very busy as we prepare to welcome guests over Christmas, decorate our homes and try to get everything done before the festive break. Luckily, the GHI is on hand to help you get ahead as much as possible before everyone descends and the madness begins. Whether that means recommending Christmas gifts, getting your spare room ready, sorting through decorations or tackling damp spots, we're here to prevent those Christmas calamities.

Declutter with
THE SKI SLOPE METHOD

Don't worry – there's no snow required to pull off this unique decluttering method, introduced by Anita Yokota in her interior design book, *Home Therapy*.

Anita, who is a trained therapist, recommends this technique to clients looking to tackle an entire room without feeling overwhelmed – the name refers to how you work your way around the space.

'The idea is to imagine your messy room like a ski slope,' explains Anita. 'If you try to go straight down, the steep angle feels scary and insurmountable. But if you traverse the slope – skiing from one side to the other – you lessen the angle and make it down the mountain without even noticing. Instead of looking at the room from front to back, look at it from corner to corner,' says Anita. In other words, declutter a single room by dividing it into small, dedicated zones and working your way across it rather than jumping around. This makes the task feel more structured and less overwhelming. It also gives you more direction as you declutter, so you do a more thorough job. And, by doing it this way, it's easier to pause and pick up again when you need to.

For instance, in your living room, you might want to start with the overflowing bookcase in the furthest corner, then move over to your dusty DVD collection on the other side, then back towards a pile of magazines on the coffee table. The important thing is not to focus solely on the clutter hotspots. Areas that require minimal effort need to be sorted too. These quick wins motivate you to keep going and make you feel like you're progressing.

Time to tidy
FESTIVE DECORATIONS

Decorations that are no longer wanted or can't be repaired should be recycled, donated or thrown away. Glass baubles aren't suitable for recycling; instead, they should go in the general waste bin — if broken, make sure you wrap them first. Plastic baubles and tinsel should go in the general waste, too. While you're sorting, it's a good idea to plug in your fairy lights and check all the lights are still working. If one goes out, the other bulbs can degrade more easily due to the increased voltage — and can also prove a potential fire hazard. Replace any broken bulbs while the lights are switched off and check they're in full working order. Store any delicate decorations in protective containers, padding them out with newspaper or kitchen roll if necessary. ◆▸

GHI HACK

Now's the time to clear out your fridge and freezer, as you'll want plenty of room for your big Christmas shop. Dispose of anything that's out of date. Take note of what you already have so you're not doubling up on anything.

Give your oven and microwave a clean before the big Christmas feast, too. Use a branded cleaner and follow the directions carefully, using gloves and taking care to ventilate your kitchen. If you want to try an eco-friendly solution, combine approximately 2tbsp bicarbonate of soda with 1tsp water to make a paste to use on the door; leave it for 20 minutes before wiping away. The shelves can be soaked in a solution of biological washing detergent before scrubbing.

Get organised

✦ The best way to store your artificial Christmas tree is in a dedicated storage bag to help protect it from damage and damp. Don't forget to recycle the old box.

✦ Try to keep decor themes grouped together and labelled, so you don't need to remove and sort through everything each year.

✦ Buy a tree skirt so cleaning up fallen pine needles from your real tree is a breeze. Unhook it once a week and compost the needles — no vacuuming required!

TACKLE DAMP

If you struggle with damp spots in your home, a dehumidifier will help eliminate excess moisture and condensation. It's particularly useful in the colder months, when it's not as easy to open windows to increase ventilation. It can also help dry laundry faster if you need to hang it indoors. Some even come with laundry modes to speed up drying times. Alternatively, a heated clothes airer is a good solution if you don't want damp washing hanging around your home.

Prepare for guests

Get ready to host visitors so they'll rate you highly for their stay! Free up space for them to store clothes in the wardrobe or drawers. Add a few hangers and a fluffy towel for each person at the end of the bed. A travel kettle with teacups and bags is another thoughtful touch.

LIFE ADMIN
Six to eight months before you travel is the best time to start planning your summer break, so book now to take advantage of early-bird deals. It will also give you something to look forward to when you get to the new year.

KEEP POSTED

Create address labels for your Christmas cards that you can use and update every year. Remember that any envelope thicker than 5mm or heavier than 100g will need a Large Letter stamp. Check when the last postal deadlines are for First and Second Class to make sure you don't leave it too late. ∎

Use winter, when the bare structure of your garden is at its most visible, to assess the landscape and see how you might improve on it. When weather permits, planting might be supplemented or plants moved to a more favourable location.

WINTER IN THE GARDEN

WHEN NATURE SLEEPS

Embrace frosty mornings and the stark beauty of winter by bringing your garden to life with colour and scent

December

1ST	2ND	3RD	4TH	5TH	6TH	7TH	8TH
9TH	10TH	11TH	12TH	13TH	14TH	15TH	16TH
17TH	18TH	19TH	20TH	21ST	22ND	23RD	24TH
25TH	26TH	27TH	28TH	29TH	30TH	31ST	

January

1ST	2ND	3RD	4TH	5TH	6TH	7TH	8TH
9TH	10TH	11TH	12TH	13TH	14TH	15TH	16TH
17TH	18TH	19TH	20TH	21ST	22ND	23RD	24TH
25TH	26TH	27TH	28TH	29TH	30TH	31ST	

February

1ST	2ND	3RD	4TH	5TH	6TH	7TH	8TH
9TH	10TH	11TH	12TH	13TH	14TH	15TH	16TH
17TH	18TH	19TH	20TH	21ST	22ND	23RD	24TH
25TH	26TH	27TH	28TH				

ACKNOWLEDGEMENTS

EDITOR-IN-CHIEF
Jane Bruton
SPECIAL PROJECTS DIRECTOR
Emma Justice

Creative Director	Marion Reilly
Art Director	Jonathan Whitelocke
Designers	Lauren Richards-Ozzati, Dan Smith
Chief Sub-Editor	Michaela Twite
Sub-Editors	Vicky Deacon, Clare O'Dwyer, Ellie Porter, Elaine Robb
Picture Director	Laura Beckwith
Picture Editor	Catherine Pykett
Picture Researcher	Jodie Anderson
News & Features Directors	Hattie Garlick, Sarah Maber
Books Director	Joanne Finney
GH Kitchen & Homes Director	Sarah Akhurst
Cookery Editor	Emma Franklin
Senior Cookery Writers	Grace Evans, Alice Shields
Style Director	Melanie Rickey
Beauty Director	Lynne Hyland
GHI Head of Content	Alison Lynch
GH and GHI Homes & Household Advice Editor	Katie Mortram
Editorial Business Director	Connie Osborne
Production Manager	Greta Croaker
Director of Business Strategy and Planning	James Hill

**MANAGING DIRECTOR GOOD HOUSEKEEPING/
GOOD HOUSEKEEPING INSTITUTE**
Liz Moseley
CEO, HEARST UK
Katie Vanneck-Smith

IMAGE CREDITS

COVER: Getty Images

PHOTOGRAPHY: David Austin, Sussie Bell, Richard Bloom, Mark Bolton, Sophie Burgham, Alun Callender, Camera Press/Grafe Und Unzer/Jalag, Mimi Connolly, Brent Darby, Annabelle Daughtry, Mike English, Heather Ford/Unsplash, Gap Photos/Joanna Kossak, Gap Photos/Howard Rice, Mike Garten, Getty Images/Istock, Annie Green-Armytage, Lorenzo Hamers/Unsplash, Jason Ingram, John Kernick, Kris Kirkham, Thomas Kuoh, Caroline Lee For The Container Store Custom Closets, Michael J Lee, Living4Media, Dan Lopez Paniagua/Arris Photography, Alex Luck, David Loftus, Becky Luigart-Stayner, Raspopova Marina/Unsplash, Malcolm Menzies/@82mmphotography, Marie Flanigan Interiors, Andrew Montgomery, Myles New, Jannine Newman, Clive Nichols, Anna Omiotek-Tott, Eugenia Pankiv/Unsplash, Michael Partenio, Ema Peter, The Picture Pantry Stockfood, Alyssa Rosenheck, Shutterstock/Rawpixel.com, Maja Smend, Ashley Smith/Unsplash, Ester Sorri/House Of Pictures, Stocksy United, Laura Streffan, Claire Takacs, Renáta Török-Bognár/Stocksy, Marcel & Jeff Wasserman/Stocksy, Stuart West, Rachel Whiting, Britt Willoughby Dyer, Brian Woodcock, Polly Wreford, Ysuel/Stock.Adobe.com

STYLING: Liz Cocozza, Emma Franklin, Jenny Iggleden, Ben Kendrick, Selina Lake, Anna Logan, Alex Mata, Jo Rigg, Alice Shields, Wei Tang, Ashley Toth, Sian Williams

ADDITIONAL WORDS: Elspeth Allison, Sophie Austen-Smith, Pattie Barron, Meike Beck, Georgie D'Arcy Coles, Gabriella English, Rachel Loos, Sarah Scherf

SPECIAL MENTIONS: Cambridge Botanic Gardens, Erin Gates, Hannah Gee, Kate Halls/@Katesinthegarden, Gemma Lewis, Hugh Lowe Strawberry Farm, Longyard Cottage, Waltham Abbey, Manor House Farm, Meleches Farm, Emilie Munroe/Studio Munroe, Ann-Marie Powell at Shepherds Cottage West Sussex, The Swedish House

Published by Hearst Magazines UK, the trading name of the National Magazine Company Limited,
House of Hearst, 30 Panton Street, London SW1Y 4AJ; www.hearst.co.uk
First published 2025

10 9 8 7 6 5 4 3 2 1